# CONTENTS
W9-BQV-277

# THE SUPER SUB™ SOLUTION

## The <u>Bible</u> of Substitute Teaching

## Charles Prosper

First Edition

Global Publishing Company • Los Angeles, California

# THE SUPER SUB™ SOLUTION

## The <u>Bible</u> of Substitute Teaching

### by Charles Prosper

*Book design and cover design by Charles Prosper*

LIBRARY OF CONGRESS CATALOG CARD DATA

ISBN  0-943845-49-1

PRINTED IN THE UNITED STATES OF AMERICA

12  11  10  9  8  7  6  5  4  3  2  1

For Melvin Powers, my mentor and life-long friend. Without your encouragement, Melvin, I would have never become a substitute teacher. You are the best, and I love you dearly.

## Chapter 11. HOW TO TEACH GIFTED STUDENTS . . . . . . . . . . . . . . . . . . . . **153**

## Chapter 12. PROS AND CONS OF LONG TERM SUBBING . . . . . . . . . . . . . . . . **155**

## Chapter 13. SUBBING STATE BY STATE. . . . . . . . . . . . . . . . . . . . . . **159**

## Chapter 14. THE FUTURE OF SUBSTITUTE TEACHING . . . . . . . . . . . . . . . **173**

*"Shoot for the moon, even if you miss, you will land among the stars."* –Les Brown

# INTRODUCTION

First of all, I want to start this introduction off with an apology, an apology for upon first glance that this book appear so "California-centric". It is not my intention to alienate all of the future subs of the other 49 states into thinking that I don't care about you as well. Subbing started out for me as a California phenomenon, and later as I really became serious and began to look at the entire United States of America, I realized that substitute teachers in every part of the country need also what I have to say. Chapter 13 is dedicated to get you started as a substitute teacher in whatever state you happen to be. I have included the departments' of education web sites and contact phone number for you to get the information that you need fast. Although not all states have a pre-requisite test before becoming a substitute teacher, some do, such as in California and New York. In Chapter 3, I talk about how to pass the CBEST test to become a substitute in California with great detail, and even though I realize that not everyone needs to take this particular test, everyone needs to know the techniques of this type of test-taking if your state is one that requires an entrance test before becoming a sub. If Chapter 3 serves you not at all, just skip it and go to the other thirteen must-read chapters.

Benefits and salaries vary greatly from state to state, with the southern states paying on the lower end, and the west coast and east coast paying on the higher end, and with all types of variation of highs and lows in between. Salaries and benefits not only vary between state to state but also between school district to school district _within each town and city_ of every state, so before you make any rash judgements or conclusions about the future of your working successfully as a substitute teacher in your area, you will need to _thoroughly_ research _all_ of the school districts within driving distance that you are willing to travel. If may be that school district that you decided not to call to be the one that pays exactly what you are looking for with exactly the teaching environment you were hoping for.

Substitute teachers change lives and help shape the future of our youth and the future stability of our country. We need more _good_ substitute teachers. Your calling awaits you. I extend my hand, and warmly welcome you to the wonderful, rewarding, challenging and fascinating world of substitute teaching.

_"It's not important that you know everything–just the important things."–Miguel de Unamuno_

*"Shoot for the moon, even if you miss, you will land among the stars."* –Les Brown

**CHAPTER**

# Why Become A Substitute Teacher

Indeed, why become a substitute teacher? I would say that if you have been musing over the idea, if teaching has always appealed to you even though you did not complete your college degree in education, I have very good news for you. Substitute teaching is the new millennium profession for *all* unemployed college graduates who like kids and enjoy imparting a most needed and valuable service.

### The Advantages of Becoming a Substitute Teacher

First of all we must understand that there is a distinct difference between a regular full-time teacher and being a day-to-day substitute teacher. (Keep in mind as you go though this list is that not *all* school districts will have *all* of the advantages.) The trick to a rewarding career as a substitute teacher is being so good and be recognized by the schools where you want to teach as reliable, responsible, dedicated and a master at classroom control. As promised, let's take a look at those <u>**Advantages**</u>:

- No Lesson Plans
- No Grading in Books
- No Correcting Tests
- No Creating Tests
- No Meetings After School
- No Having to Call Parents
- No Obligation to Work Everyday
- Health Benefits
- Life Insurance
- Home Loan Benefits
- Work 7:30 – 3:30 (Monday through Friday)
- Saturdays and Sundays Off
- Take A Vacation (Unpaid) Any Time You Want
- Free to Promote to Any School That You Wish
- Free to Study for a New Career at Night
- You Don't Have to "Take the Job Home with You"
- You Can Earn from $22,000 – $42,000 a Year
- Get Paid for a 6.6 hr. Workday
- Get Special Perks Afforded Only to Teachers
- Start a Part-Time Home-Based Home Business

*"Think you can, think you can't; either way, you'll be right."—Henry Ford*

Once we take a look at each one of these advantages in detail, we'll see if you can resist this great opportunity after *really* seeing the full picture:

### Advantage #1: No Lesson Plans

Having worked as a long-term substitute teacher which is the equivalent of being and doing all of the things a regular full-time teacher does but for only a 30-day period, I have learned that one reason why you are paid slightly more to do long-term subbing is for all of the unexpected extra time at night you will suddenly find yourself expending doing such routine chores as lesson plans. Lesson plans take time. You will usually have to prepare for two or three days at a time to give yourself somewhat of a better vision where you want to take your class for that week. Be prepared to spend at least one or two hours to thoroughly plan for your classes a night, especially if you are teaching subjects which might require experiments or projects. These one or two hours that you spend preparing for classes is time taken away from your family or other pursuits. As a substitute teacher on a day-by-day basis, while you are playing with your daughter in the evening or pursuing some hobby or leisure activity in the late afternoon, there is somewhere a regular teacher preparing a lesson plan for you. Advantage #1 of being a substitute teacher is No Lesson Plans.

*"Genius is an infinite capacity for taking pains."–Jane Ellis Hopkins*

### Advantage #2: No Grading in Books

Regular full time teachers as well as long-term subs have to record all of the grades in the record books of all 150 - 240 students that they may have for the 5 to 6 periods that they may have. In most large metropolitan public schools, there are usually 30 to 40 students per classroom. (Yes, schools <u>are</u> overcrowded!) So just do the math:

40 students  x  6 periods  =  240 students total

When you record grades in the books, you will have to grade on a weekly, monthly, midterm and final grade end-of-semester basis *for all of your students.* This is <u>very</u> time-consuming! If you calculate and enter into the records books each student's grade which is what you will have to do, and if to process the grade of each student takes you, say, only 3 minutes, then how long do you think you will spend at grading–even if you happen to be using a grading software program and are not entering each final grade by hand?

240 students  x  3 minutes  = 720 minutes
720 minutes  =  12 hours of grading

Advantage #2 of being a substitute - No Grading in Books!

## Advantage #3: No Creating Tests

If you are a regular full-time teacher or if you are doing long-term subbing, guess who has to regularly create all of the tests. You guessed it. You do. To properly evaluate and grade a student's work and performance, you should give a quiz or test of some sort at least 3 times per week. The tests that you administer must be coordinated to test the learning goals of your lesson plans. Creating tests requires careful thought and preparation such that they are fair and are able to adequately measure that which you have taught. After you have created the master test, you now have the chore of making enough copies, usually something that you can do in the copy room of your school, staple the sheets together and organize them by periods. As is often the case, you may be teaching, during any given track, two or more compatible subjects, such as math and science, or English and social studies, or Spanish grammar and Spanish literature. This means that you now must consider having to create two sets of tests, copying them and organizing them. This all goes with the territory of a regular full-time teacher, but as a sub, this is Advantage #3 - No Creating Tests.

*"Mediocrity knows nothing higher than itself, but talent instantly recognizes genius."–Arthur Conan Doyle*

## Advantage #4: No Correcting Tests

Once you create a test, administer it to your students, you now have the chore of correcting each, one-by-one, and entering their scores into your grade book. There are basically two types of tests that you will correct and grade; they are the multiple choice type or fill-in-the-blanks type of test **or** the essay/analysis type of tests. Ideally the best type of test to administer from a time-saving perspective would be a type of test where any helper, (a teacher's aide, spouse, volunteer student) with the aide of an answer key, could assist you in grading, but there will always be those tests which require critical thinking and a type of response that *only* the teacher him or herself must correct. But wait! You don't have to worry about this–you're a substitute teacher! Advantage #4 - No Correcting Tests.

## Advantage #5: No Meetings After School

I heard a regular full-time teacher once say, "If an administrator could not call a meeting, they would not have anything to do." I would not go far as to say that, but I will say that as a regular full-time teacher, be prepared to attend plenty of departmental meetings, professional development meetings, new policy change meetings and meetings as to why there are so many meetings. These meetings usually take place after school. I have attended a few of these meetings and though necessary, it is not the most edge-of-your-seat experience that you could think of. Depending on who the speaker is and the subject matter, they can be anything from very interesting to excruciatingly boring. Regardless of how you find these meetings on the scale of interest and excitement, they are an additional chore that consumes part of your day. As a sub, this is your Advantage #5 - No Meetings After School.

### Advantage #6: No Having to Call Parents

José Meza just started a fight again in your class. He is flunking your course, and he shows no signs of improvement even after repeated visits to the school counselor's office, detention and verbal warnings of school suspension. The only recourse now is to call the parents, or is usually the case, call the parent, and arrange an after-school or during-your-conference-period-during-the-day, parent/teacher meeting. These type of meetings can be very productive or very frustrating as it is very common that if a child has gotten to that stage of disorganization and mental disarray it is more often that not a sign of the absence of authority, guidance and values at home. Some parents come and are in total agreement with everything that you say, but have somehow relinquished their job of guiding and controlling their child and have left it up to the school, teachers and administrators. Other parents are in total denial and are utterly defensive of whatever their little brats do to consistently disturb and interrupt the class and the teacher. These parents blame the teachers and the school for their child's ills, and are sometimes even offended that a teacher may have to raise his or her voice at their "little darlings". Whatever the case may be, you, dear future sub, will not have to deal with this at all. You have Advantage #6 - Not Having to Call Parents.

*"Nothing great was ever achieved without enthusiasm."–Ralph Waldo Emerson*

### Advantage #7: No Obligation to Work Everyday

Let me tell you that there are going to be times when you just don't want to go in. You don't want on this day, for whatever reason, the grief, the stress, the yelling. This is normal. Even <u>regular</u> full-time teachers feel like this and very frequently feel the need to take off. (Actually, this is where you step in as a substitute teacher.) But, if the day comes that you really feel the need to take a break, a day of rest, just do it. Take a day or two off. Don't accept anything for today and tomorrow. Go to the beach. Drive out to the countryside with your family. Go see an early matinee movie. Sleep late. Watch Jerry Springer. Call in for pizza. Go to the library. Read a good book. Do whatever it is that you need to do to relax and rejuvenate yourself before going in to sub for another day. Remember, as a substitute, you have the luxury of deciding how many days and how frequently you would like to work. Full-time regular teachers don't have that same ease of when and how frequently they can be absent. They <u>do</u> take off, we both know that, or you as a sub, could not exist. The difference is that <u>you</u> can easily do it with little consequence because you are the owner of Advantage #7 -

No Obligation to Work Everyday.

### Advantage #8: Health Insurance Benefits

When I talk to full-time regular teachers, there seems to paint a look of disbelief on their faces when I tell them that some substitute teachers receive all the same health insurance benefits as they do. Yes, that's right! In *many* major city school districts (and I admit in not all), providing that you work a minimum of, say, three days a week to total, for example a minimum of twelve days a month during any given pay period, you, dear substitute teacher, will receive all the same emergency hospital care, co-pay doctor visits, vision and dental insurance plans that full-time regular teachers receive–*for you, your spouse and your kids!* When you sign up to work for the school district in your area, be sure to ask about their health benefits. Thus, now armed with this knowledge, prepare to enjoy Advantage #8 - Full Health Insurance Benefits.

*"Well begun is half done."–*
*Aristotle*

### Advantage #9: Life Insurance Benefits

Depending on which school district you are working in, as a substitute teacher working a minimum number of days per week, you *may* also receive full life insurance benefits. Should you leave this earth unexpectedly, your designated beneficiaries will receive whatever insurance benefits to take care of your final resting place as well as leave them with whatever sum of money that you have chosen among the life insurance plans available to you. (You should first always check with your school district's substitute unit's benefits department to determine how many days per pay period that you need to work subbing in order to maintain all of your benefits.) Worry not about coverage if you are the beneficiary of Advantage #9 - Full Life Insurance Benefits.

### Advantage #10: Home Loan Benefits

Did you know that there is a federal program through the U.S. Department of Housing and Urban Development (HUD) to help teachers who are first time buyers to purchase their home with little or no down payment and with very, very low interest rates, and a relaxation of the stringent credit requirements that most traditional banks and mortgage companies will ask for. One such program is called "The Teacher Next Door" (TND) which offers single family homes to public school teachers (which also includes *substitute teachers* who work on a *full-time* basis, that is 4 to 5 days a week) with the following benefits:
- 50% discount off appraised value
- Only $100 Down payment required if the home is purchased with a FHA insured mortgage

The down side of this program is that it is never a house in the best area of your town. Nevertheless, if you are living in a area already where

HUD housing is found, you can move from being a renter to a home owner with very little effort and lots of help from the U.S. government. At the time of this writing, the web site were you may find more information about this program if you are interested is:

`http://www.fha-home-loans.com/teacher_next_door_fha_loans.htm`

For many, this can be Advantage #10 - Full Home Loan Benefits.

### Advantage #11: Work 7:30 – 3:30 (Monday through Friday)

Ever heard the term "banker's hours"? This expression comes from the time when bankers worked from 9:00 a.m. to 2:00 p.m. Well, working as a substitute teacher would not quite qualify as banker's hours, but it comes darn close to all of the conveniences of regular hours at the most convenient time of day. Just think, you go in for 7:30 a.m., and your day ends at 3:30 p.m. Compare this to most corporate jobs out there of the 9:00 – 5:30 variety. Even worse, consider the hours of any manager at almost any retail location of any chain store. Hours in the morning alternating with hours in the evening. Don't discount the possibility of graveyard shifts, and of course working on holidays. It is oh so sweet to be able to finish your day in the mid-afternoon, and be able to plan the evening any way you wish. Go take in a movie. Take out a friend or your family to dinner. Go to the gym and workout. Regularity in work schedule is a premium advantage. In this case, it is Advantage #11 - Work 7:30 – 3:30 (Monday through Friday).

### Advantage #12: Saturdays and Sundays Off

The beauty of the weekend is having Saturdays and Sundays off. I know of many people at a variety of jobs whose days off never fall on the same two days, let alone the same two days back-to-back. To me, having Saturdays and Sundays off is sort of like expecting each work week to end with a mini-vacation. Because we are substitute teachers, at any time that we need or wish, we can take off Friday, Saturday and Sunday. Saturday, Sunday and Monday. Or a trip to see the family on a Friday, Saturday, Sunday and Monday. Let us celebrate Advantage #12 - Saturdays and Sundays Off.

### Advantage #13: Take a Vacation (Unpaid) Any Time You Want

As you observe from above, the natural extension to having Saturdays and Sundays consistently off is the you can creatively append a couple of days on either the Saturday or the Sunday side of the weekend or both and take yourself a mini-vacation. Keep in mind that these are unpaid vacations, but if you set aside regularly money for you to take off every once in a while, the fact that it is unpaid pales in comparison to the freedom and exhilaration that you can feel in being able to decide when _you_ want to take off and relax. So, every once in a while, go

_"See things as you would have them instead of as they are."–Robert Collier_

ahead and enjoy Advantage #13 - Take a Vacation Any Time You Want.

### Advantage #14:  Free to Promote to Any School That You Wish

Consider this for a second.  A full-time teacher accepts a position at a given school only later to find out that the school is poorly administered, is in a high crime area, and the students as a whole are the most disrespectful and rebellious that you could ever imagine.  Well, as a new full-time teacher, you are pretty much locked into that school for a while.  You cannot capriciously change schools from one day to the next after making a commitment to teach full-time at a certain location.  Your references are not going to look too good in terms of reliability from the principal of the school that you ditched.  However, as a substitute teacher, should you discover the same situation above, the solution is easy.  You would not accept any more jobs from that school, and just go about the business of promoting yourself at a more favorable school, a place where you would *love* to teach!  You see, while a regular full-time teacher who has just accepted a position has to contend with just that school, as a substitute teacher, you usually have at your fingertips *dozens* of schools that you may choose from within your chosen area.  And in most cases you also have the option of changing your *area* as well whenever you wish.  Only subs have easy access to Advantage #14 - Free to Promote to Any School That You Wish.

### Advantage #15:  Free to Study for a New Career at Night

Let us take a step back a bit and revisit Advantage #11 – Work 7:30 – 3:30 (Monday through Friday).  There is only one possible way to study for a new career at night and that is you have some regularity of day work schedule.  Maybe substitute teaching is a way station for a different career goal that you have set for yourself.  I know many actors who have broken into film while working as substitute teachers by day and going to acting school at night.  I know of singers, musicians and artist who attribute their success to the wonderful work schedule of substitute teachers.  Maybe you want to become a computer programmer, a graphic artist, a medical technician...a butcher, a baker, and yes, even a *candlestick maker!*  If you can dream it, plan it, and study for it at night–you <u>can</u> become it with the help of Advantage #15 - Free to Study for a New Career at Night.

### Advantage #16:  You Don't Have to "Take the Job Home with You"

At most jobs, we have to see and deal with the same disagreeable and difficult people on a daily basis.  Some of us dread the fact the another Monday morning marks the challenge of having to repeat a toxic environment.  You don't have to "take the job home with you", because who you have to deal with:  kids, teachers and front office people can change

*"I think and think for months and years.  Ninety-nine times the conclusion is false.  The hundredth time I am right"–Albert Einstein*

7

from day to day and from school to school. Remember, because of all of the schools that you have available to choose from, you are never locked into any one school environment forever. If you had a hard day with a tough group of kids on any given day, you don't have to necessarily deal with them the next day (unless you have accepted a long term position–and even *that* is temporary.) Therefore, you don't have to anguish over any particular day because tomorrow is a fresh new beginning. Accept now Advantage #16 - You Don't Have to "Take the Job Home with You".

### Advantage #17: You Can Earn from $22000 – $42,000 a Year

How much can you make as a substitute teacher is a question that I get all of the time. Well, this depends a great deal on where you are teaching. Some cities and school districts will pay more than others. For example, here in Southern California where I reside, a substitute teacher working in middle upper-class Mission Viejo, California will earn $90.00 a day, while the same substitute teacher working in Metro Los Angeles, California will make as much as $172.00 per day. Why such a difference? Well, the demographics and the type of students that typically can be found along with budget allocations are the determining factors. In some areas of Los Angeles such as in South L.A. and East L.A, you are going to find some of your toughest customers in the student body. And when I say tough customers, I am referring to discipline problems of the escalated type in some situations. Defiance, profanity, disrespect and rebelliousness is not uncommon. I have even heard of some teachers refer to the extra money that they are making as "combat pay." Whatever the reason is there will be a pay scale difference from city to city and school district to school district.

Let's break it all down. Annually there are:

$$52 \text{ weeks } \times 5 \text{ days a week } = 260 \text{ days possible}$$
$$-14 \text{ holidays}$$
$$\overline{246 \text{ total work days}}$$

$$246 \text{ days a year } \times \$90 \text{ a day } = \$22,140 \text{ a year}$$
$$246 \text{ days a year } \times \$172 \text{ a day } = \$42,312 \text{ a year}$$

Of course the secret is to be able to teach every possible work day available without fail. Impossible? Not at all. With the never-before-revealed secrets of self-promotion that you will learn later on in this book, not only will you be able to work every possible day that there is to work, you will also learn how to be able teach in only one or two preferred schools that *you* have chosen! You will soon have at your fingertips Advantage #17 - You Can Earn from $22,000 – $42,000 a Year.

*"Life is too short to read bad books."–Charles Prosper*

### Advantage #18: Get Paid for a 6.6 hr. Workday

In most school districts, you will get paid per hour based on either a 6.6 hr. workday or a 6.0 hr. workday. Let me elaborate and show you how interesting this gets for a substitute teacher. As mentioned earlier, you will get paid differently respective to the area and school district that you choose to work in. If you are working at a school that pays you $90.00 per day, you are making $13.64 per hour. If you are working at a school that pays you $172.00 per day, you are making $26.06 per hour. Though the workday schedule varies slightly from school to school, a *regular bell schedule* might look like this:

7:24 a.m. – 3:19 p.m.

This means that your total regular work day will comprise itself of 7 hours and 55 minutes. But do you really work 7 hours and 55 minutes? Not always. There is a lot of gracious free time built into each of these regular work days. At most schools you get a break to each for Nutrition for 20 minutes at about 10:00 a.m. (The idea behind Nutrition is that many kids by having to get up so early to get to school in the morning oftentimes will skip breakfast which, as everyone knows, is the most important meal of the day and is a cause of lack of mental performance if there is no nutrition intake until the noon lunch; this is also good for *teachers* who skip breakfast to get to work on time.) You also get a 30-minute lunch at about 12:30 p.m. In addition to all of this, you can get, if you are not called to cover someone else's class, an 60-minute conference period which is an hour of free time for you to do as you wish. (The theory behind a conference period is that all regular full-time teachers need a free disposable hour during the day to: see parents, counsel problems kids, catch up on grading papers or to create tests; *you inherit this free hour* as part of that teacher's schedule for whom you are substituting.) So if we add up all of the hidden free time that you are given, you have 1 hour and 51 minutes – *almost 2 hours of free time at your disposal!* In actuality, you *work* only 6 hours and 4 minutes on a typical regular day such as this! But wait, it gets sweeter, there is something called *Professional Development Days* which many schools have adopted where every, say, Tuesday or Thursdays, the school schedule is something like:

7:24 a.m. – 1:37 p.m.

This is a 4 hour 31 minutes school day! You still get paid for 6.6 hours as long as you stay in the library or the teacher's lounge until 3:19 p.m. The theory behind Professional Development Days is to give regular teachers on a weekly basis ways to hear wisdom and innovative sugges-

*"We cannot direct the wind, but we can adjust the sails."–Anonymous*

tions of administration. You have to miss all of the excitement of these meetings and must entertain yourself with a good book or just relax in the lounge. Could it get any better than this? Yes! There is something called *Minimum Days* where the school's schedule is as such:

7:24 a.m. – 12:34 p.m.

There are those days during certain times of the year, such as those that are close to the beginning of a holiday or the at the beginning or the ending of a new teaching track where your day is only 4 hours and 4 minutes. This 4 hours and 4 minute work day (as well as the Profession al Development Day) is calculated based on the nutrition, lunch and conference periods where you don't have to teach. In the case of the Minimum Day schedule you will deduct a 25 minute brunch and a 41 minute conference period that you are given. Isn't substitute teaching wonderful! Why? Because you get to enjoy Advantage #18 - Get Paid for a 6.6 hr. Workday.

### Advantage #19: Get Special Discounts Afforded Only to Teachers

My wife loves specials. Anytime someone says discount or whatever percent off – she's there! I'd never been much of a coupon clipper or bargain shopper, but once I became a substitute teacher and began to see the perks and discounts of my profession, I became a born-again bargain-boy! This book that you are holding in your hands now was written in part by a loaner laptop that I was able to get from the computer department of the middle school where I work the most. Let me explain how this is possible. After you have selected the school where you want to work the most, and after you have executed your self-promotion strategy with artistic grace and skill, you probably have become a familiar face at that school assuming that you have managed to work there 3 to 5 times per week. Now it is time to get to know the head of the computer department, the person who issues out loaner laptops for the use of the regular teachers there. Drop by and visit him or her. Introduce yourself and take an interest in his or her computer department, and engaged them in a conversation about their wonderful computers and allow them to brag and talk about all of the subjects that are typical of a computer-phile (like *myself*). Be a good listener. Be an interested listener. Let them show off to you their knowledge and their department. People love to be listened to. Giving someone your undivided attention is a compliment *(and a rarity)*. Giving your undivided attention to another human being gives that person (every person–even me) what they want the *most*–and that is a *feeling of importance*. After you have spent a pleasant time talking computerese, you leave and say thank you for the information. You not only say thank you for the in-

*"There is no such thing as a problem without a gift... you seek problems because you need their gifts."–Richard Bach*

formation when you leave, but you also, on the same day leave a Thank You note of the variety that you buy in the business stationery department of stores like Staples®, Office Depot®, or Office Max®, the ones that are blank and allow you to write in any personalized message that you wish.  Inside the blank portion of this Thank You note, you will write "Mr. Lee, thank you so much for the informative explanations that you gave me of the computer equipment and the programs. I really appreciate it." – *Mr. Whatever-You-Name-Happens-to-Be.*  In addition to this Thank You note, to put this technique on steroids, you place a $5.00 lunch gift certificate to a popular chain food eatery in your area such as SubWay®, El Pollo Loco® or Quizno's Sub®.  You get the idea.  What do you think that computer department director's reaction to you will be after *this!*  Can you say *Wow!*  Now don't go back the next day and ask for a laptop.  Allow a few more weeks of more conversation and friendship to develop.  Then and only then, after you have established a relationship do you ask Mr. Lee, "Mr. Lee, as you know, I am pretty much a regular here at this school.  I am here practically everyday.  I have several projects for school that I would like to develop using a computer.  Do you think that it would be possible for me to get a loaner laptop from the computer department?"  If Mr. Lee has the final word on who gets a laptop and who does not, trust me, you *will* have your loaner laptop.

Let us say that after you use the school laptop for several months, you would like to purchase your own.  Well, you can, and there is no need for you to pay full price.  Teachers, all teachers, including substitute teachers are afforded special discounts by being associated with any recognized public school in the United States.  Apple Macintosh at `apple.com` offers deep discounts (hundred's of dollars) off of the regular retail costs of all of their computers.  If you are into amusement parks and rides, entertainment centers, such as Chuck E. Cheese's® and the like, teachers can get special discounts from these as well.  Check with your school to see what all of the special discount items that are available.  Advantage #19 - Get Special Discounts Afforded Only to Teachers.

### Advantage #20:  Start a Part-Time Home-Based Business

Some teachers only want to teach, and this is very noble thing.  But as a substitute teacher, your sights may be set on *more* than just teaching. There is absolutely no reason why you cannot, in addition to your substitute teaching, start a part-time home-based business.  I have had an import/export internet business as well as an internet Spanish translation business for years in addition to my substitute teaching.  It is the easiest thing in the world to have a home-based business in addition to substitute teaching.  With a home-based business, you can increase your yearly income by an additional $5000 – $12,000. This means that if you are earning $22,000 a year or $42,000 a year as a substitute teacher, with your own business, you can earn as much as $34,000 a year or $54,000 a year working only part-time in the evenings when you get off of work in the afternoon. Actually, you can make much, much more than that, depending on what your goals are and the part-time business that you choose. If the idea of making extra income and creating financial independence for yourself sounds appealing for you, then there may be a budding entrepreneur trying to come out and express him or herself. For ideas on which home-based businesses which might be right for you, I would suggest that you pick up and read magazines such as *Entrepreneur* and *Business Income Opportunities* that you would find at your local newsstand. Another way to self-discovery of finding the right home-based business for you is to pay attention to the late night informercials that offer business opportunities. My bottom line suggestion when selecting a business for yourself is <u>not</u> to make how much money you can potentially make as the main criteria for choosing a business. You have to choose something that you would <u>love</u> to do regardless of the money. This is the only attitude and energy that will allow you to continue when things go wrong in the initial stages of the learning experience. Do what you love, and the money will follow. Be about the business of providing a useful service to your fellowman, and be about the business of increasing the quality of life of another, and money, riches and prosperity will flow into your life in amounts that you cannot measure. Advantage #20 - Start a Part-Time Home-Based Business.

*"All you need is a plan, a road map and the courage to press on to your destination."–Earl Nightingale*

### Advantage #21: Test the Waters Before Going Full-Time

Let me step back a bit. Let us assume that you recognize your calling, your only calling, to become a full-time credentialed public school teacher. Fine. But let me show you how to go about doing it. Before you go after and pursue a full-time career as a teacher, my strong suggestion is that you do whatever it takes to make yourself available for and to take a long-term substitute assignment of at least 30 days with the same class. This means that you will have the full experience of what it is to have the responsibility of one group of kids on a daily basis. You will have the opportunity: to create your own unique variety of lesson plans, to create evaluative tests, to do grading, to counsel students and to talk to parents. You cannot go wrong with Advantage #21 - Test the Waters Before Going Full-Time.

*If* you have decided <u>not</u> to go full-time, and rather as many SuperSubs have opted to do, to become a *career* substitute teacher *indefinitely* and to eventually *retire* from substitute teaching, you will often get this question from regular full-time teachers who notice that you are requested practically everyday at a particular school "Why don't you work full-time?" Most full-time teachers cannot or will not understand the mind set of a SuperSub. We _don't_ want to grade papers, see parents, do reports and attend endless administrative meetings *ad nauseam* and take lots of work home to spend an extra hour or two which can be spent with family or other interests. (We can almost make the same amount of money as full-time teachers as we have already explained.) Quite frankly, I think that some full-time teachers even resent the idea that we want the _benefits_ of teaching but not the _burdens_ of teaching. But that just the way things are. Substitute teachers are freer, fuller and fabulous entities. Whenever you are asked the question about why you are not working full-time, don't try to explain why. It will fall on deaf ears. If you try to explain (justify) your *raison de etre,* you will only be seen as unwilling to commit to a "_real_" teacher's position. Just bypass the question with something to the effect that you still need to take more credential courses to qualify, and leave it at that. _We_ know why you do what you do. Nod. Nod. Wink. Wink.

*"Your life is only as good as the people you serve."–Charles Prosper*

*"Shoot for the moon, even if you miss, you will land among the stars."* —Les Brown

# The 10 Big Lies of Substitute Teaching

Every profession or field of study has its facts and fallacies. As with anything else, substitute teaching has developed its own set of myths and misconceptions. No, let's call a spade a spade. Some of these misconceptions are just *down right lies.* There are 10 big lies which surround substitute teaching that I would like to dispel right now and once and for all.

*"Not everything that is faced can be changed, but nothing can be changed until it is faced."–James Baldwin*

### The 10 Biggest Lies About Substitute Teaching:
- Substitute Teaching is Not as Stable as Full-Time
- Substitute Teachers Never Get Insurance Benefits
- Substitutes Aren't as Dedicated as Regular Teachers
- Substitute Teachers Teach Only Certain Subjects
- Substitute Teachers are Not "Real" Teachers
- Substitute Teachers Cannot Control the Classroom
- Substitute Teachers Always Earn Less than Full-Time
- Substitute Teaching is Not a Career
- Substitute Teachers Secretly Yearn for Full-Time
- Substitute Teachers Do Not Positively Change Lives

### Lie #1 Substitute Teaching is Not as Stable as Full-Time

*Fact :* Good substitute teachers, once they are recognized as such, are *never* out of work! And I mean *never!* Good substitute teachers are *always* in demand! Teachers will literally fight over you if you are a good sub.
    –"I asked him *first!*"
    –"No, you didn't! *I* did!"
And so the dialogue goes. Once teachers at your chosen school really get to know you, you will have to turn away many times multiple requests to teach on the same day. Now factor in that you may also promote and become well known at more than two or three schools, you will have enough work to book yourself for job opportunities as much as two months in advance. Also, the longer you are a substitute teacher, the more you'll be called by the Sub Desk of your school district. With all of this work-

working for you, you will be working 5 days a week with no problem. So, let us lay this myth to rest once and for all, substitute teaching is as stable as regular full-time teaching. If you can consistently manage to work 5 days a week, what more stability could you ask for?

## Lie #2   Substitute Teachers Never Get Insurance Benefits

*Fact:* As long as you are working a minimum amount of hours per school year, you can qualify for full benefits. For the Los Angeles Unified School District, by way of example, you need a total of 600 hours of service a year to qualify for full medical, dental and vision benefits. What this breaks down to is a minimum of 4 1/2 months a school year, or in simpler terms, you would need only to work an average of *2 days a week* for full coverage. 600 hours per school year is usually enough service to qualify you with most school districts. You will be able to get all the same health, dental, vision and life insurance benefits that is afforded to full-time teachers. Before you let any uninformed person talk you out of your justly deserved insurance benefits that are available for you *and your family,* you should call the benefits department of your school district and get all of the *facts.* School districts *need* good substitute teachers, and they are willing to do whatever it takes to keep them – which means offering full insurance benefits.

## Lie #3   Substitutes Aren't as Dedicated as Regular Teachers

*Fact:* Substitute teachers in the grand majority *are* dedicated to what they do as much as any regular teacher. By the fact that certain subs are called in and requested on a daily basis is a testament to their reliability and reputation. There exists a type of haughty undercurrent of superiority to substitute teachers on behalf of *certain* regular full-time teachers – for whatever reason there may be. It is a sad fact that though they *depend* upon us to take care of their classes when they are out, some teachers have an abject distrust for subs. As I heard about one teacher, from the mouth of one of his students, on the day that I was called in to sub for him that, quote: "All subs ever do is come in and screw up everything." That's unfortunate, for this mentality does exists, and maybe even in the minority, but it *does* exists. The perception is that

*"There's a way to do it better...find it."–Thomas Edison*

unless you have committed to full-time, you are a second-class teacher. When I teach, I care that the kids learn what it is that I am teaching, and I will do whatever it takes to ensure the integrity of the class for all those that are there to seriously get an education.

## Lie #4   Substitute Teachers Teach Only Certain Subjects

*Fact :* A good substitute teacher is capable of teaching *all* subjects whichever they may be. The fact is that most teachers leave lesson plans which are easy to follow. Those who don't leave lesson plans is still no cause for worry – as you, as a SuperSub, always have at your disposal a briefcase of emergency lessons plans on any subject which you are to teach.

## Lie #5   Substitute Teachers are Not "Real" Teachers

*Fact :* We teach. We discipline. We affect lives. If we are good enough and dedicated, we help inspire the best that there is in every student. What else is this but a "real" teacher?

*"Be like the eraser...forever forgiving."–Charles Prosper*

## Lie #6   Substitute Teachers Cannot Control the Classroom

*Fact :* Substitute teachers know more about instant classroom control than regular teachers. You see, the difference between a substitute teacher and a regular teacher is that a substitute teacher has only a matter of minutes to establish his or her authority, develop rapport and command immediate respect. A regular teacher has had weeks if not months to develop this authority, rapport and respect. We do it instantly! We *have* to do it instantly! Regular teachers who are off track for a couple of months and want to make extra money opt to sub at other schools. They are often dismayed to discover that what they took for granted in their ability to control a classroom is put to the test when they have to do it in a sub environment of instant classroom control. If a good sub can't control a class within the first few minutes of beginning – then *who*?

## Lie #7   Substitutes Always Earn Less than Full-Time

*Fact :* Substitute teachers can earn from $22,000 – $42,000 a year depending on the amount of days worked per week (4 – 5 days) and the school district for which you work.

## Lie #8   Substitute Teaching is Not a Career

*Fact:* I have been a substitute teacher going on 8 years. I know of substitute teachers that have been substitute teaching for as much as 15 years. They have families, homes, nice cars and vacations. They have money in the bank and investments. They teach 4 to 5 times a week and love what they do. If this is not a career, I don't know what is. Substitute teaching can and is a career if you choose and want it to be.

## Lie #9   Substitutes Teachers Secretly Yearn for Full-Time

*Fact:* This myth is usually perpetuated by those who don't understand the benefits of substitute teaching and the mindset of the professional career sub. Substitute teaching is fulfilling in and of itself, and in the mind of the career sub, there is no secret yearning to go full-time.

## Lie #10   Substitute Teachers Do Not Positively Change Lives

*Fact:* All concerned and caring teachers touch all lives in a powerful and positive way if there is love in the heart of the teacher. I cannot count the number of times students have come to me in private for counseling to reveal things to me that they felt that they could not reveal to anyone else. I recall the day when I was teaching life skills to a class of about 12 students. I was teaching them how to set goals and how to discover their life's purpose. I explained that discovering what you should be doing in life is not based on how much money some careers or professions are purported to earn, but rather on choosing one's profession in life based on asking the right questions. I said to this group of edge-of-their-seat listeners that the wrong question is "How much money does this or that profession pay?". The right question to ask is "What profession can I choose that will allow me to provide the greatest service to the greatest number of people while using my special talents, gifts and abilities?" Following this new perspective there was an engaging question and answer period where creativity and enthusiasm flowed all over the room.

The most poignant and moving point of this class was when I mentioned that I am a former children's social worker and counselor, and that I had to work with cases of rape of little girls by their fathers. I dimissed the

*"Fact is a disguise of faith."–Charles Prosper*

class.  All of the students left out of the class thanking me for my insights.  One girl, aged about 18 years old, a senior in this particular high school, stayed behind.  She was in tears.  I asked what was the matter.  She confided to me that when she was 7 and again 13 years old that her father secretly raped her repeatedly over long periods of time then fled to Mexico.  Her mother never wanted to believe her until it was too late.  She explained that she has never been able to relate to a boyfriend as she would always break up whenever sexual involvement started.  I sat there with her, and we looked up on the internet free and low cost counselling clinics in her area that specializes in her problem.  She eagerly wrote down the information.  There was a sense of relief in her eyes and gratitude that cannot be expressed in words.  I don't know what became of this young lady following the day of that class, but I would be bold enough to say that I left a permanent, positive impression on her.  May God bless her wherever she is!

*"The mind is the limit.  As long as the mind can envision the fact that you can do something, you can do it, as long as you really believe 100 percent."–Arnold Schwarzenegger*

*"Shoot for the moon, even if you miss, you will land among the stars."* –Les Brown

**CHAPTER**

# How to Past the CBEST™

I n order to be a substitute teacher, in certain states, such as California, Oregon or New York there are qualifying tests which you must pass in order to make you eligible. One such test is called the CBEST™ which stands for California Basic Educational Skills Test. ("CBEST" is a trademark of the California Commission on Teacher Credentialing and National Evaluation Systems, Inc. NES®.) The purpose of the CBEST™ is not to measure or evaluate your effectiveness as a teacher, but rather it is an assessment test of your proficiency in reading, writing and mathematics. In this chapter I will explain what the CBEST™ consists of and certain fail-proof techniques that will guarantee that you pass it easily. (If you reside in another state other than California, like Oregon or New York, this chapter still may be very useful to you. Even though the CBEST™ is a test pertinent to California, the test-taking techniques that I show you in order to pass this test would be the same test-taking technique for any similar qualifying state exam that consists of math, reading and writing.)

*"Kids take play very seriously."—Charles Prosper*

## Who Must Take the CBEST™

If you are applying for your first teaching credential, applying to be a day-to-day sub, or if you have not taught in a school district for the last 39 months, then the CBEST™ will be a requirement for your employment. The fee to take the exam is reasonable. It is $41 for what is considered regular on time registration, but it gets a little more expensive depending on whether you are a procrastinator or last-minute type of person. Late registration is an additional $20 if you allow to pass a certain cut off date, and you pay an additional $40 if you, say, wait until the day before the date of the test to register. To register, contact:

**CBEST Program**
National Evaluation Systems, Inc.
P.O. Box 340880
Sacramento, CA 95834-0880
(916) 928-4001 9:00 a.m. - 5:00 p.m. (pst.)

There is also a web site for more information on the test. Go to:
http://www.cbest.nesinc.com

## What *is* the CBEST™

The CBEST™ is a four hour test that tests you on reading, mathematics and writing. Prior to August 1995, you had only these four hours to complete all three sections which meant spending 65 minutes for the reading, 70 minutes for the mathematics and 60 minutes for the writing. To attempt to do all three facets of testing in the same fours is grueling and thoroughly exhausting. Things have changed, and now you have more flexible and creative use of your time. Now, you can take the reading, the math and the writing on three separate dates, and on each separate date, *you can take the full four hours* for each subject! This is the *smart* way to do it! Sure, you'll have to pay another $41 to register for each section, but trust me, it is well worth the investment.

The CBEST™ is given six times a year. A typical ***test dates and registration*** schedule might look like this:

| Test Date | Regular Registration | Late Registration | Emergency Registration | Score Mailing Date |
|---|---|---|---|---|
| **Aug. 9, 2003** | July 11, 2004 | July 29, 2003 | Aug. 5, 2003 | Sep. 3, 2003 |
| **Oct. 11, 2003** | Sep. 12, 2004 | Sep. 30, 2003 | Oct. 7, 2003 | Nov. 3, 2003 |
| **Dec. 6, 2003** | Nov. 7, 2004 | Nov. 25, 2003 | Dec. 2, 2003 | Jan. 5, 2004 |
| **Feb. 21, 2004** | Jan. 23, 2004 | Feb. 10, 2004 | Feb. 17, 2004 | Mar. 15, 2004 |
| **April 17, 2004** | May 19, 2004 | April 6, 2004 | April 13, 2004 | May 10, 2004 |
| **June 19, 2004** | May 21, 2004 | June 8, 2004 | June 15, 2004 | July 12, 2004 |

*"I start where the last man left off."*–Thomas Edison

Now don't forget that the regular registration is $41. If you pay on the late registration date, you pay $61, and if you wait to register by the emergency registration date, you pay $81. (Keep in mind also that emergency registration is limited to selected areas and to availability.) If you want immediate toll free automated information available 24 hours a day, call 1 (800) 262-5080.

There is no limit to the number of times that you can take the CBEST™. If you take the exam again, you don't have to repeat the sections that you have already passed. A passing score is 51.25 percent for each section. Even if after taking your test, and for some reason you feel that your performance on that day is not representative of what you consider your best, you can cancel your CBEST™ test score by letting the supervisor know that before you leave the room. When your score is mailed out to you, you are the only person who receives it. No one else gets it. The NES (National Evaluation Systems) will also mail your scores to specific schools if you request them on your registration form.

There is one final requirement to becoming a substitute teacher and obtaining your teaching credential. You must also have a least a bachelors of arts, a B.A. degree, on any subject.

Indeed, why are substitute teachers different from regular full-time teachers? There are many reasons why that the average person has not even begun to think about. Let us take a look at just a few of the distinctions of this special breed of teacher:

## Barron's How to Prepare for the CBEST™

Absolutely, positively the only study guide you will ever need *Barron's How to Prepare for the CBEST™* published by Barron's Educational Series, Inc. The ISBN (International Standard Book Number) is the number your local bookstore uses to quickly find a book for you; have it handing when you call and inquire of availability. The ISBN for *Barron's How to Prepare for the CBEST™* is 0-8120-9731-9. It sells for $14.95, and is the best study guide of the lot of study guides that are available. In it is has not only explanations and techniques on how to pass the test, but also gives you plenty of real practice tests that imitate perfectly the real thing. When you have practiced and passed enough of the exercises in the book, the reading, math and writing sections, you will have *no* problem in passing the real CBEST™.

## The 7 Success Secrets for Passing the CBEST™

*"It is one thing to write poetry, yet another to be called a poet. It is one thing to write, yet another to be called a writer."–Charles Prosper*

I have always said that nothing is difficult if you know what you are doing, and there is power in simplicity. The next seven steps that I will give you here have both the elements of showing you how and in the simplest way imaginable. There are only seven secrets to passing the CBEST™ which are:

- Take the Three Test Sections on Separate Dates
- Take Five-Minute Breaks Every Forty-Five Minutes
- Take Water, Juice, Finger Sandwiches and Fruit
- Complete Practice Exams Before Taking the CBEST
- Eliminate Any Social Activities or Stressful Events
- Go to Bed Early the Night Before the Exam
- Take Time to Review All Answers When You Finish

Assuming that you have already purchased and have been to study and practice with *Barron's How to Prepare for the CBEST™* study guide, let us take a closer look at each of these seven test-taking success secrets.

## Secret #1 - Take the Three Test Sections on Separate Dates

It has been mentioned elsewhere in this book, but it is worth repeating that the number one secret to taking and passing the CBEST™ is to take the reading, the math and the writing sections of the test on three separate dates. Instead of exhausting yourself with trying cram all three sections in one four-hour period, allow yourself the luxury of taking *each section* in complete four-hour periods. Doing math requires a different part of your brain than doing analytical reading or evaluative essay writing. When you exhaust one part of your brain, say, the math side, it is very difficult to shift gears and empty the energy banks from the reading and writing side or vice versa. It is extremely tiring and stress to do all three parts in the same four hours. It is do-able but at great wear and tear on your mental perspicacity and alertness. Therefore you are now armed with the Test-Taking Success Secret #1 – Take the Three Test Sections on Separate Dates.

### Secret #2 - Take Five-Minute Breaks Every Forty-Five Minutes

A dear teacher of mine taught me years ago that whenever you are intently working at anything over a long period, it is never wasted time to rest. In fact, the wisest thing that one can do is to rest *before* he or she gets tired. With this secret number two, it is assumed that you are taking each of the three sections of the CBEST™ separately, that is, you are allowing yourself the full four hours for the reading, the math and the writing on different dates. With this beginning strategy in place, you will take a break of 5 minutes every forty-five minutes. The way it works with the CBEST™ is that you may take as many breaks as you wish. This only means that you are taking time from your own testing. However, since four hours is more than enough time to finish subjects on a individual basis, you can plan to take up to five 5-minute breaks every 45 minutes. What you do it is that you take your test materials up to the test supervisor and leave it with him or her while you go out. They will always say yes. You are now headed to the restroom and then for a nice place on the outside to sit and have an nutritious snack and a refreshing drink.

### Secret #3 - Take Water, Juice, Finger Sandwiches and Fruit

To prepare yourself for your regenerating rest periods during your testing, you must have your provisions ready. The night before, you prepare: finger sandwiches, fresh fruit slices, juice and bottled water. Your finger sandwiches allow you to snack on small portions. Fresh fruit is best place in Tupperware® type of containers. You juice and water should be placed in bottles. If you are expecting it to be hot on the testing day, do yourself a favor and freeze your water in the bottle, and let it slowly melt during the day so that you can have ice cold refreshing water. All of this snacking is designed to last under 5 minutes, just enough for your mind and body to fully recuperate for the next forty-five minutes. While you are outside, take your mind away from the testing. Enjoy the fresh air. See the trees. Hear the birds chirping. Feel the breeze. This is test-taking the way God intended it to be! Five minutes may not sound like a lot, but when it is planned for in this systematic way the regenerative effect is cumulative and powerful. You may even intensify the relaxing effect by reading book of inspiring

*"Wisdom is knowing what path to take next...integrity is taking it."–Anonymous*

quotes while you munch and slurp. Breathe deeply and let go. Then get up and go back into the test room with that noticeable glow of readiness.

### Secret #4 - Complete Practice Exams Before Taking the CBEST™

Having purchased the study guide *Barron's How to Prepare for the CBEST™*, the goal is to study and practice the exercises with the idea of completing the practice exam just as you will experience it on the day of the test. Even it wouldn't be a bad idea to take a four-hour period, and go to your nearest public library, and practice each part of the exam (on three separate days) *with* your finger sandwiches, juice, fruit and water, breaking every forty-five minutes for five minutes. At your five-minute break time, you take up your materials, go to the restroom, then go outside for your finger sandwiches and a sip of juice an/or water. You will be able to experience beforehand the effectiveness of this incredibly regenerating test-taking technique. Test-Taking Success Secret #4 is Complete Practice Exams Before Taking the CBEST™.

### Secret #5 - Eliminate Any Social Activities or Stressful Events

What are you planning to do the night before the date of your exam. Go out dancing? Don't do it. Help your brother-in-law move into his new house? Postpone it. Stay up a little late watching *The Untouchables* with Kevin Costner. Don't do it. You must avoid any activity that will exhaust, tired, overstimulate or excite you. The way you go to sleep is the way that you will wake up. Therefore heed Test-Taking Success Secret #5 – Eliminate Any Social Activities or Stressful Events.

### Secret #6 - Go to Bed Early the Night Before the Exam

Plan to get up very early, and to get up wide awake and refreshed. The only way that is going to happen is if you are in bed no later than 9:00 p.m. Avoid any heavy meals after 7:30 p.m. Once awake, you will have breakfast, bathe and have plenty of time to arrive an *hour* before the test is scheduled to start. Even if you are a chronic procrastinator, *force* yourself to wake up leave out early enough to arrive an hour ahead of time. Set the alarm. Not having to rush is a great stress-reliever. Test-Taking Success Secret #6 is Go to Bed Early the Night Before the Exam.

### Secret #7 - Take Time to Review All Answers When You Finish

You have brilliantly planned and flawlessly executed your strategy. You have easily finished the exam with still another hour to go. Don't discard the luxury of this last hour without carefully reviewing and checking all of your answers when you have finished. After you have thoroughly reviewed your answers to satisfaction, leave with confidence.

*"Your happiness is just on the other side of your fears. Can you cross over?"–Charles Prosper*

*"Shoot for the moon, even if you miss, you will land among the stars."*–Les Brown

**CHAPTER**

# How to Prepare for a Day of Subbing

B e it your first day or your fifty-first day, you need a success routine for preparing yourself for a day of subbing. My suggestion is to establish this preparation ritual early in your substitute teaching career so that success becomes second nature. After looking over mentally my many years of substitute teaching, I think that I can condense the day's preparation into 7 success tips.

*"We will either find a way or make one."–Hannibal*

### The 7 Success Tips to Prepare for a Day of Subbing:
- Prepare Your Lunch the Night Before
- Select and Lay Out the Clothes You Will Wear
- Arrange Your Emergency Lesson Plans in a File
- Have Driving Directions to All of Your Schools
- Lay Out Your Business Cards and Thank You Notes
- Lay Out Your Videos, Desk Lamp and Ear Plugs
- Go to Bed by 9:00 p.m. and Wake Up by 5:00 p.m.

### Secret Tip #1 - Prepare Your Lunch the Night Before
Were you *really* planning on eating in the school cafeteria? There are several very good reasons why you should prepare to take your own food every day. When you prepare and take your own food, :

1) You are saving from $2.50 to $5.00 per day considering the fact that at most schools you have two opportunities to eat, once at about 10:00 a.m. which is called Nutrition and lasts for about 20 minutes. The other opportunity we all know as Lunch, served traditionally at 12:00 p.m or 12:30 p.m., and this lasts for about 30 minutes.

2) The food that you prepare will always be better than school cafeteria food unless you are into grease.

3) You save 5 to 10 minutes of your nutrition or lunch time because the school cafeteria is a very popular place for teachers and the lines are very long. No long lines for you!

### Secret Tip #2 - Select and Lay Out the Clothes You Will Where

Am I making too much common sense here? Well, that's all this is. But it is in the simplicity of life that the beauty of life is revealed to us. All of my suggestions revolve around reducing as much stress for a day of subbing as possible. Substitute work can be very stressful at times by its nature in and of itself. There is no need to add unnecessary and extraneous stressors. Having to rush and make last minute decisions is a great stressor. This reminds me of a very good substitute teacher whom I've known for over four years whom I will leave nameless, but if he ever reads this, I know that he will recognize himself. This sub manages to *always* run late. He is *always* in a hurry to get out of the door because he consistently lacks to take the time to prepare himself the night before. I have seen him come to work with Bermuda shorts and funky T-shirts because to quote him, "I didn't have time to shave or take a bath this morning." Can you believe that this was sometimes the topic of his lunch-time conversation? Some people has very serious procrastination issues, and it allowed to run wild and take control of some of the vital and important aspects of your life can be definitely considered neurotic and self-defeating behavior. One sure way to conquer procrastination is to *force* yourself into healthy self-perpetuating *routines*, such as simply selecting and laying out your clothes the night before. Do this every night for 21 days and it will become a habit and a saving grace.

*"Solutions depend on how you define the problem."–* Charles Prosper

### Secret Tip #3 -Arrange Your Emergency Lesson Plans in a File

I was once asked in an interview on how to become a SuperSub, and the question was posed to me, "What if a sub goes in to a class and there are no lesson plans, then what do they do?" My answer was that this is not the mindset of a SuperSub. A SuperSub would never walk into a class–a SuperSub would never *think* of walking into anyone's class without a briefcase of emergency lesson plans. The reality is that not all teachers will have a lesson plan all nice and neatly prepared for you on the desk. There *will* be times when there will be *no* lesson plans, and this is not always due to any indifference or ineptitude on the part of the regular teacher. It may be just because the teacher woke up that morning sick and was not able to leave a lesson plan for you.

When you first accept employment, you are asked what are the subjects that you are willing to teach. Whatever subjects you place, (and you *should* place *all subjects* because a good sub *can* and *should* be able to teach *any* subject for a day), you should have at least a half dozen or so ready-made and neatly typed out lesson plans for that subject. As you meet regular teachers and sub for them, copy and use some of the best lesson plans that you see which could in a generic sense for any other class that you might teach on that subject.

Another way to obtain and excellent lesson plans on every subject is from the internet. Just go to your favorite search engine, such as Google.com:

**http://www.google.com**

Type in the search box something like, English, lesson plans, middle school, *and voilà*–pages upon pages of beautiful lessons all for the asking done by teachers experts in the field. You should do this for every subject that you plan to teach and specify if it is middle school or high school. Use your desk drawer or any type of file box to store away the master sheets. When you are called to go in to sub in the early morning, the computerized call from your Sub Unit will indicate the school and of course the subject. Once you accept and hand up the phone, go to your files and pull out the master lesson plan sheets for that subject you are being called in to teach on that day. Because you will arrive early enough to the school (Right?), you will have time to go in and make enough copies for your first two periods if you arrive to the room and notice that there are no lesson plans. If you can't manage to make the copies that you need in the morning before class, you can always send a student from your class with a note to the copy room and have someone make the necessary copies for you because of the lack of lesson plans. Don't forget that some lesson plans may not require that you make a lot of copies. Some lesson plans may require that the students do the majority of the writing with the proper focus. At any rate, the bottom line is that you *never,* and I mean never, *ever* walk into a classroom without some sort of emergency lesson plans that you have brought in from home. If you do, I will deny that you ever read my book.

### Secret Tip #4 - Have Driving Directions to All of Your Schools

Most school districts will have a resource booklet that lists all of the schools in their domain. My suggestion is to request and to get a hold of this comprehensive list to decide exactly which are the schools where you plan to accept work as a substitute. Once you have made you list, place them one by one on 3" x 5" index cards with the name of the school, the address, the city and the phone number. It is also vital to place the name of the contact person in main office who in charge of filling the sub vacancies of each school. (Later, you will see that this person will be your key person and "*best friend*" to get you a continuos stream of more sub jobs for that school. More on this in the chapter on self-promotion.) After the above information has been carefully placed, *on the back of each index card,* write down the fastest street or freeway route to get there. Take the time to go over and study each route before placing them in your index card file box. When that phone rings calling you in to work. You will know exactly how and where to go.

*"The love of life is necessary to the vigorous prosecution of any undertaking."–Dr. Samuel Johnson*

29

## Secret Tip #5 - Lay Out Your Business Cards and Thank You Notes

I am getting a little ahead of myself here in talking about business cards and thank you notes as this will be part of the grand subject in a later chapter on The Secrets of Self Promotion, but here I will begin to whet your appetite with covering the importances of laying out these two important items out to take with you the next day. You will learn how to professionally make and design your business cards announcing your availability as a substitute teacher. After creating these stunning business cards, you will then place them in the hands of the teachers and the main office ladies who will be able to call you when needed again and again. You will also learn how to prepare blank thank you notes, those type which you find in the stationery section of your office supplies superstore like an Office Depot, Office Max or a Staples. Inside of these blank thank you notes, you will write the messages that are directly to the teachers for whom you sub as well as place a business card. The point of this section is to explain to you that you should have at least a dozen business cards and thank you notes in your briefcase and ready to go when you leave out of the door. At the end of each day of work, you will leave a thank you note and a business card in the desk of the teacher you are subbing for as well as on the desk of the mail office ladies who help you the most in getting you to your class and helping whenever you need it.

*"We cannot direct the wind, but we can adjust the sails."–Bertha Calloway*

## Secret Tip #6 - Lay Out Your Videos, Desk Lamp and Ear Plugs

It's funny, but just today I was called in by the computerized sub desk to sub for a Spanish teacher. When one is called, there is a place where a teacher will leave special instructions for the class. Today the message was that there would be a movie for the students to watch and take notes on in order to complete it for homework. Knowing that I was going to see the same video for each of the five periods, I decided not to bored myself with the same film over and over again for hours. When I know that I will show a movie, I always take in my trusty desk lamp. Students usually expect you to turn out the lights, and I usually do unless the class is really rowdy. Once you are in the dark, you are bound to only watch the movie again and again and again. After seeing the film once in the day, I find it most productive to pull out a good book and read it while the movie is going on at my desk. Even though in the dark, my black desk lamp from home, makes this possible. Sometimes the movie gets a little loud or by its nature, it is very distracting. No problem. As long as I am facing the students and watching carefully their behavior, I can easily muffle out 85% of the movie's noise to allow myself to read comfortably and without any major distractions by simple placing foam ear plugs inside my ears, the kind you get at any drugstore. If a teacher is not having the class watch a video, it is always a good idea to carry a couple of good general and instructional videos in your briefcase according to the subject matter of the class. This way if you walk into a classroom without any lesson plan, you can always request a VHS and television and make it your instant lesson for the day. For science, Bill Nye, the Science Guy is great for science classes. The famous claymation series of Wallace and Gromit is excellent for English classes to study characters and plot while thoroughly enjoying the movie. The Disney classic, *Donald Duck in Mathematics Land* is excellent for math classes at all levels. Stick with "G" rated movies only to keep yourself out of trouble with the administration. And of course, you should not forget that the school's library is a wealth of great videos which you can borrow for a day under the teacher's name for whom you are subbing.

### Secret Tip #7 -Go to Bed by 9:00 p.m. and Wake Up by 5:00 a.m.

With this secret tip #7, I don't know if I am asking something that is reasonable or outrageous. This will all be based on your pass sleeping and waking habits. Whatever the case may be, you are entering the real world of subbing. Your first calls from the sub unit start as early as 5:20 a.m. Remember, that night-before preparation and getting up early means that you will be free from the pressures of much to do with little time to do it. The last thing that you want to do is to wake up sleepy without enough sleep, or worse yet, wake up late *and* without enough sleep. You need to be at the top of your mental focus. Fatigue is a self-inflicted enemy. Rest and relaxation are you greatest allies.

One more thing, if you for some reason find that you are running later, always give the main office a call to let them know that you are on your way. If you call and let them know that you are running late, they will have a teacher to cover your first period for you until you arrive. If you don't call them and let them know what's happening, you run the risk of their assuming that you will not arrive, and they may cancel you job and call the sub desk for another sub to go in instead of you. This happened to me by experience, and I dutifully learned my lesson. I was called in to sub in an area that was far away from where I live and in an area that I was not familiar with. To make a long story short, I got lost, and I arrive *an hour late!* That I arrived an hour late was not as bad as that I hadn't called to let them know that I'd got lost and that I was on my way. The school was about an hour away from my home. When I got there, the main office worker told me, *"Oh, Mr. Prosper, I just canceled your job number, and another sub is on the way to replace you. We're sorry, but we had no idea if you were going to show up or not."* Though a little miffed because of all of the distance that *I* chose to travel, after thinking about what happened from an objective perspective, I could only admit that I was wrong and they were right.

*"Shoot for the moon, even if you miss, you will land among the stars."*—Les Brown

# Emergency Lesson Plans Made Easy

The most basic technique for handling any class that you walk into without any lesson plans is to quickly ask the nearest and most intelligent looking student, "What is the text book that you use for this class?" and then, "What is the last page of the lesson where you left off?" With this information, you quickly scan the following lesson and any exercises that you find in the book. Once you get the essence of what they are learning, you came proceed to teach a lesson on the fly. Any good substitute teacher can and should be able to do this. In this lesson, I am going to go beyond the simple advice of above and share with you proven lesson plans that you can add to you emergency lesson plans file. The following lesson plans were shared with me by some of the most brilliant minds in teachings. My thanks go infinitely out to them. I will cover lesson plans for 6th through 8th grade (**Middle School**) and 9th through 12th (**High School**). I will offer for you lesson plans on five major subject categories.

## The 5 Major Subject Categories for Emergency Lesson Plans:

- **English**
- **Social Studies**
- **History**
- **Math**
- **Science**

Before I go into giving you the actual emergency lesson plans, don't forget your other emergency lesson plan basics. If there is no lesson plan left for you in the room, assuming also that you have arrived in the class early at least thirty minutes before the bell, look around the classroom and see if you can find a TV and VHS player. If you don't see one, immediately quick with one of the regular teachers next door to find out where you might obtain one before the class. The idea is that you have with you at least two ready educational videos that would be appropriate for the subject. If you don't have a good video for the subject you are going to teach, this is what you can do. You can send a trustworthy-looking student with a note to the school library asking the librarian to select a couple of good video titles for you to use in the class to be checked out under the regular teacher's name, explaining who you are and that you will return the videos back today. Before starting the video, explain that they will take notes and write a summary to hand in.

## Lesson Plan #1 - English Language Arts (Middle and High School)

**TITLE:** HOW TO KNOW YOURSELF AND OTHERS THROUGH POETRY

**SUMMARY:** Aside from being an interesting and ready-to-execute lesson plan, this is also an excellent tool to open channels of communication and trust with students who have difficulty expressing themselves, even and especially those students who are at risk of failing and/or dropping out. You provide an open atmosphere for improving their self-concepts as well as the medium to use and improve writing skills.

**GRADE LEVELS:** 6th through 12th. Middle School and High School.

**GOAL:** For you to get to know students quickly and to get students to know themselves better and more lucidly through writing. Students also become more familiar with word usage, the use of synonyms and the various degrees of emotion contained in certain words and how to manipulate language to impact the semantics of meaning.

*"Any man can get what he desires provided he's willing to pay whatever price."–Arnold Schwarzenegger*

**RESOURCES & MATERIALS:** The only materials required for this exercise is an open mind, a willingness to do it and paper and pencil.

**ACTIVITIES & PROCEDURES:** You adroitly begin a discussion with them about what exactly are feelings and emotions. Have each student take out a sheet of paper and pencil and write down a word which describes how he or she is feeling today. Use this sentence:

Today I feel **(name of emotion)** because **(give reason)**.

Explain to them that it is very possible to have more than one emotion or feeling at the same time which can be either similar or the complete opposite.

**EXAMPLES:**

Today I feel **(worried)** because **(we are having a test)**.
Today I feel **(happy)** because **(today is Friday)**.

Now you will help students to examine their emotions more closely. Have students number their paper 1 to 10 in a vertical list order. Have them then brainstorm a list of any 10 emotions; they can be good or bad or an combination of both. Now, and this is very important; ask the students to choose only *one* of the ten emotions that they have written down. Here comes the fun part. Ask the students to assign a **color** to their chosen emotion, and write down a short sentence. Examples are:

"Hate is **black.**"   or   "Happiness is **yellow.**"
Have them explore further with the next phase of the exercise.  Have they write down and model the following example of sentences using their particular chosen emotion:

| (Emotion) is (Color). | Fear is **red.** |
|---|---|
| It smells like_____. | It smells like **burnt matches.** |
| It tastes like_____. | It tastes like **rotten apples.** |
| It feels like _____. | It feels like **a bad toothache.** |
| It sounds like_____. | It sounds like **growling dogs.** |
| It looks like _____. | It looks like **vampire fangs.** |

The next phase of this exercise is to create with the chosen emotion a metaphoric statement.  For example:

**(Fear) is (give a metaphoric statement).**

**"Fear is falling into a hole."**

Now, following the above exercise, they are equipped to effortlessly create a Bio-Poem (Biography Poem).

**Bio-Poem:**

| Line 1 | Your first name only |
|---|---|
| Line 2 | 4 traits that describe you |
| Line 3 | Sibling of...(or son/daughter of) |
| Line 4 | Lover of...(three people or ideas) |
| Line 5 | Who feels...(three items) |
| Line 6 | Who needs...(three items) |
| Line 7 | Who gives...(three items) |
| Line 8 | Who fears...(three items) |
| Line 9 | Would like to see...(three items) |
| Line 10 | Resident of...(your city, street or state) |
| Line 11 | Your last name only |

**Example:**

Kayla
Shy, bubbly, happy and energetic.
Daughter of Melvin and Marcia
Lover of volleyball, orchids and cheerleading.
Who feels happiness with friends, loneliness at night, and joy
at ball games.
Who needs friends, love and acceptance.
Who gives friendship, love and encouragement.
Who fears pain, death and losing family.
Who would like to see the world, the future and never-ending joy.
Resident of Los Angeles, California
Powers.

*"You may be disappointed if you fail, but you are doomed if you don't try ."–Beverly Sills*

35

## Lesson Plan #2 - English Language Arts (Middle School)

**TITLE:** LET'S GO SHOPPING AT THE MALL

**SUMMARY:** This is a lesson involves observation, role playing, writing through the eyes of a character, and making a presentation to the class. Students will visualize themselves as an observer humanity in a certain situation. They will step out of their own character and not the character of someone else. They will react to certain situations as they imagine someone else might, and then they write about it. You may need to reorganize your classroom a bit to simulate a shopping mall which this in itself they will love to do. You need no special equipment or materials.

**GRADE LEVELS:** 7th through 9th. Middle School

**GOAL:** As the wonderful lesson unfolds, students will begin to understand how they observe, identify and oftentimes judge someone else by that person's behavior and appearance.

*"Proscrastination is the thief of time."–Edward Young*

**RESOURCES & MATERIALS:** The only materials you will need for this activity are a flexible room, lots of imagination, a very heavy book, an improvised microphone, paper and pencil.

**ACTIVITIES & PROCEDURES:**

1. Go up to the board, and ask students to brainstorm with you the different "types" of people they might see at a large shopping mall on a busy Saturday afternoon (families, kids, security and custodial people, clerks, retired people, "mall walkers", people trying to sell you something as you pass by stores, etc.) List as many as possible on the board.

2. Have the students choose one of the characters, and visualize what that character might be doing at the mall. Now adjust your classroom to accommodate movement and have the kids actually simulate their characters by turning the room into the shopping mall! Encourage the kids to really get into their roles.

3. After the students have been role playing for about two minutes, make sure they are completely absorbed in what they are doing–then–*slam* the heaviest book in the room down on the floor! They will all have a startled reaction. Explain that a huge explosion has just occurred. Instruct the students to return to their desks and write what just happened from the point of view of the character that they are pretending to be.

**4.** Now have them all go back to their seats and write what has just happened–*from the point of view of the character they are pretending to be.*

**5.** Allow the students five to ten minutes for them to write their papers, and then ask them to form small groups of four to five students each to read their writing to each other. Each group should choose the "best" or most effective writing from their group.

**6.** You select a TV interviewer from the class and stage a MAN ON THE STREET interview with all of the selected authors. It is probably a good idea to choose one of the least successful of your writers to boost his or her self-esteem in the process.

**7.** The writing is followed by a discussion on how they look at each other and how different people might have differing perspectives on the same experience.

## Lesson Plan #3 - History (Middle School)

*"Chance does nothing that has not been prepared before-hand."–Alexis de Tocqueville*

**TITLE:** THE ORIGINAL THIRTEEN COLONIES

**SUMMARY:** It is a rare opportunity for students to learn some of the creative memory mastery techniques often taught in some of the most expensive paid training seminars for adults. Using the thirteen original colonies as the focus of this instant memory exercise, they will learn two important things: the names of the thirteen original colonies, in order, but most importantly, they will learn a memory mastery technique that will be useful for them the rest of their lives.

**GRADE LEVELS:** 7th through 8th. Middle School

**GOAL:** As a result of this activity, the students will know and be able to effortlessly say the thirteen original states *and* the order in which they entered the Union. The students will really enjoy learning these 13 states. This memory exercise is best done after discussing the Constitution and its ratification.

**RESOURCES & MATERIALS:** No special materials are necessary.

**ACTIVITIES & PROCEDURES:**

**1.** At the beginning of the class period, you will announce to the students that they are going to play a fun game. *(Just say the word game, and you will get their full and undivided attention!)*

**2.** Starting with a person in any row, ask that person to repeat and imagine the structures you are proposing to build. Challenge the rest of the class to see if they can visualize these things as each student repeats them.

**3.** Tell the first student to visualize and to repeat out loud the word *"Corningware dish."*

**4.** Move to the second student, and have him to imagine many chopped-up pencils in the Corningware dish. Have this second student to describe in detail the scene which he is now visualizing for the entire class.

**5.** Ask the third student to visualize a new-born Jersey calf standing on the above described chopped-up pencils that are inside the Corningware dish. Ask him to repeat all of the information up until this point starting with the Corningware dish, then the chopped pencils and now with the Jersey calf standing on top of it all.

**6.** Everyone knows someone named "George." Have the next person, the fourth person, imagine a friend named George riding on the new-born Jersey calf that was just described above. Now ask this student to recite the whole list starting from the first item: Coringware dish, chopped-up pencils in the dish, a new-born Jersey calf standing on them and George riding on the calf.

**7.** The next student, the fifth one, is now told to imagine that George is holding onto a disconnected radio. (Encourage the students to embellish with all of the elaborated or exaggerated detail that they wish, just as long as they remember the essential part of each step.) Ask this student to remember and then to repeat all that has been accumulated, namely, the Corningware dish filled with chopped-up pencil, the Jersey calf standing on the pencils and George riding on the calf and holding a disconnected radio.

**8.** The following student, the sixth one, is told to imagine that on the disconnected radio is a mass of tangle wires. Have him or her repeat from the beginning that there is a Corningware dish holding chopped-up pencils supporting a new-born Jersey calf being ridden by George who is holding a disconnected radio with a tangled mass of wires on top.

**9.** The seventh student is told to think of someone they know who is named Mary. (Who doesn't know a Mary?) The student is then asked to imagine this person named Mary with her feet all tangled up in mess in the tangled mass of wire, and visualize that she is

*"Experience is the best teacher, after you have read and studied it in a book."–Charles Prosper*

looking all around trying to find a place to land in case George drops her. The student must again repeat step-by-step verbally what has accumulated.

10. The eighth student is asked to imagine a friend named Carol. Carol is sitting on Mary's shoulder and wearing a skimpy bikini. Again have this student to recite the complete list up until Carol.

11. The ninth student must imagine that Carol is not too clean in her hygiene as she is now holding in her hand a new, bloody ham that is very slick. Have student number nine to recite the entire list including the new item of the new, bloody ham that is very slick.

12. The tenth student must envisage that on the slick ham is standing a girl named Ginger (or Virginia) who is trying to maintain her balance. Have this student review and recite the whole list now including Ginger (or Virginia).

13. The eleventh student must imagine that Ginger (and Carol and George) is tough enough to carry the Empire State Building. This student then recites the list.

*"Men don't fail, they only stop trying."—Anonymous*

14. The twelfth visualizes that Carol is a magician and that this time she is sitting on top of the Empire State Building. However, because she is so high, this time she is wearing a fur coat. Once more, the student must reiterate the entire list up until now.

15. The thirteenth and final student must imagine that, at the very top of this structure, a big Rhode Island Red rooster is sitting on Carol's head. The student must finally repeat the entire list. Allow as many other students who would also like to repeat the entire list to do so.

After the game is over, ask if anyone in the class would be interested in learning the 13 original states and the order in which they entered in the union. Most will not be all that enthusiastic by saying that it is too hard. Then tell them that they have already just learned it. They will give you a puzzled look at this point. See if anyone can figure out where you are leading them. If none are able, just give them the translation code below:

1. Coringware dish      - Delaware
2. chopped-up pencils    - Pennsylvania
3. new-born Jersey calf  - New Jersey
4. George                - Georgia
5. disconnected radio    - Connecticut
6. tangled ~~Mary~~ Mass     - ~~Maryland~~
                           Massachussets

| 7. | tangled Mary | – Maryland |
| 8. | Carol in a bikini | – South Carolina (hot south) |
| 9. | new bloody ham | – New Hampshire |
| 10. | Ginger (or Virginia) | – Virginia |
| 11. | Empire State Building | – New York |
| 12. | Carol in a fur coat | – North Carolina (cold north) |
| 13. | Rhode Island red rooster | – Rhode Island |

After reciting successfully the list, get into a meaningful history lesson of the thirteen original states. Finish off the lesson by asking one more person to successfully give the thirteen states and in the correct order. Your students will never forget you for such a great and entertaining learning lesson.

## Lesson Plan #4 - History (Middle and High School)

**TITLE:** HOW TO FORM A GOVERNMENT

**SUMMARY:** The formation of a government and the development of laws is a concept that is taught form the beginning to the end of school. This lesson helps students to understand the systems of government, a the laws that they create and the punishments assigned for the violation of those laws. Though the use of a cooperative learning activity the students will develop their own government, author laws and designate the consequences for the violation of those laws.

**GRADE LEVELS:** 7th through 12th. Middle School and High School.

**GOAL:** The skills that the students will develop are many as a result of this lesson are many.
1. Cooperative learning *skills* as they will have to work together just like in real life.
2. Leadership skills as some one in the class will have to take charge.
3. Law related skills as they will have to make up their own laws and consequences for violations of those laws.
4. Written language skills as everything they do will need to be recorded. They may even write their own constitution.
5. Geography skills as they will have to find out where they are.
6. Imagination skills as this is a skill of utmost importance in each and every significant endeavor that we undertake.

**RESOURCES & MATERIALS:** No special materials are necessary.

*"The deed is everything, the glory nothing."–Johann Wolfang von Goethe*

**ACTIVITIES & PROCEDURES:**

This lesson finds students on an island after their ship has wrecked, or their plane has crashed. Food, fresh water and shelter are in short supply. The students must form a government, develop laws and penalties.

1. Choose a place and a period in time for the student to crash or wreck on the island.

2. Inform them that food, water and shelter are in short supply. They will also need to know that their chance to be rescued is zero.

3. At the end of the activity they will be required to turn in the following written work:
   a) A description of the type of government that they have chosen.
   b) A list of laws that the new government has developed.
   c) A list of the penalties for violation of these laws.

4. Explain to the students that during the activity the teacher will be grading each student on his or her own participation.

5. Develop a self-evaluation for the students which is a very important step as this will be the best record of what the students have learned.

6. Let them go at it, and don't interfere. (It's best if you start with a set time frame and then work from there.)

7. When they have finished, discuss the outcome as a group.

Let the students work as a group – they may surprise you. In the discussion at the end of the lesson, have the students evaluate their laws and the punishments that they have assigned them. See if they feel the punishment fits the crime. You as the teacher may want to relate the students' penalties to those assigned to our laws. If the class has assigned the death penalty as consequence, this can open a whole new area for discussion. The design of the lesson is to take advantage of those teachable moments. Let the students lead for a little while, and you will be amazed at what you can teach them, and conversely, what *they* can teach you.

*"In basketball and in life, you'll always miss 100% of the shots that you don't take."–Charles Prosper*

## Lesson Plan #5 - Science (Middle and High School)

**TITLE:** CRASHED ON THE MOON

**SUMMARY:** This is a group activity that can be used in

Earth-Space to make the differences between the environments on the earth and the moon more relevant, and to set the stage for our study of the basic environmental differences between the earth and other planets.

**GRADE LEVELS:** 7th through 12th. Middle School and High School.

**GOAL:** Students memorize the environmental differences among the planets but usually do not develop a feel for how they might affect life in that environment. This lesson stimulates a student's thinking about what their life might be like on the moon and then sets the stage for a brief study of the environments on other planets. Students will as a result of this lesson be able to compare and contrast the environments of our moon and the earth. Give practical examples of how these differences might affect one's activities on our moon.

**RESOURCES & MATERIALS:** A script of the spaceship crash, and the list of survival equipment available on the spaceship.

**ACTIVITIES & PROCEDURES:**

1. The teacher of students who have done the necessary research, compare and contrast, both verbally and in writing, some of the major environmental differences between the earth and our moon. Examples of some major factors are:
   **a.** Atmospheric Pressure
   **b.** Temperature
   **c.** Weather
   **d.** Gravity
   **e.** Organisms
   **f.** Oxygen Available
   **g.** Crustal activity - quakes, volcanoes & movement

2. Examples are solicited from other students about how these differences might affect daily activities on our moon from the class.

3. Students are then divided into groups. Each group is the crew on a spaceship that is about to crash on the moon.

4. They usually read a prepared script describing their "crash"

5. Following the crash, an announcement is made that the spaceship is disabled; the radio is broken, and the nearest base is 50 kilometers away. Each group must get to the base with no outside help.

6. Their task is to decide as a group which emergency supplies from their disabled spaceship to take with them.

*"It wasn't raining when Noah built the ark."–Howard Ruff*

They are to list the supplies in order of priority and state why they chose each item.  Below is a partial list that is usually given:

- First Aid Kit
- Water
- Freeze Dried Food
- 50 Feet of Rope
- Parachute
- Inflatable Raft
- Small Backpack Stove
- Stove Fuel
- Matches
- Standard Backpack Tent
- Sleeping Bags
- Pressure Suit
- Extra Oxygen Cylinders for Pressure Suits
- Compass
- Map of the Moon
- Suit Repair Kit
- Flashlight

*"Scoundrels are always sociable."–Arthur Schopenhauer*

Afterwards, each group reports on their list and why they chose each item.  The teacher of the students in charge discuss the "official list" and why the items were prioritized as they were.  There are no real right and wrong answers although some items would obviously be more valuable on the moon in an emergency.

Students compare and contrast the environmental differences found on the earth and the moon on paper. They give examples of how each difference might affect their life if they were living on the moon.

The teacher uses this activity to introduce the study of the environments of the other planets.

## Lesson Plan #6 - Math (Middle School)

**TITLE:**  EASY ADDITION

**SUMMARY:**  This lesson gives students who are having trouble with CARRYING and ADDITION problems or simply this is for students who are slow when adding, who want to add faster and more accurately, and students who want to add without pencil and paper.

**GRADE LEVELS:**  6th through 8th.  Middle School

**GOAL:**  Upon completion of this lesson, the students will be able to add correctly and quickly.

**RESOURCES & MATERIALS:**  Paper, pencil and addition problems.

**ACTIVITIES & PROCEDURES:**

Here is the lesson:

**1.** Problem –
```
     35
   + 24
```

**2.** Add from LEFT TO RIGHT (the OLD way is to add the ONES first then carry.)

Add the TENS first
```
     30
   + 20
   ────
     50
```

Then add the ONES
```
      5
   +  4
   ────
      9
```

Then add the answers
```
     50
   +  9
   ────
     59    NO CARRYING
```

**TIP:** Start with problems that require NO carrying (when using the OLD method) so that they get the idea, and then progress to more difficult problems as seen below:

| | Steps | (1) | (2) | (3) |
|---|---|---|---|---|
| **EXAMPLES:** | 378 | 300 | 70 | 8 |
| | + 958 | + 900 | + 50 | 8 |
| | ──── | ──── | ──── | ──── |
| | 1200 | ← 1200 | | |
| (4) | 120 | ← 120 | | |
| (Add) | 16 | ← 16 | | |
| | ──── | | | |
| | 1336 | **THE ANSWER!!** | | |

| | Steps | (1) | (2) | (3) | (4) | (5) |
|---|---|---|---|---|---|---|
| **EXAMPLES:** | 5830 | | 5000 | 800 | 30 | 0 |
| | 2967 | | 2000 | 900 | 60 | 7 |
| | 836 | | | 800 | 30 | 6 |
| | + 38566 | + 30000 | + 8000 | + 500 | + 60 | + 6 |
| | ──── | ──── | ──── | ──── | ──── | ──── |
| | 30000 | ← 30000 | | | | |
| | 15000 | ← 15000 | | | | |
| (6) | 3000 | ← 3000 | | | | |
| (Add) | 180 | ← 180 | | | | |
| | 19* | ← 19 | | | | |
| | ──── | | | | | |
| | 48199 | **THE ANSWER!!** | | | | |

**TIP:** If the above example had a list of sums that ended with a 20* (rather than 19), the list can be added just as the original problem was added so that the student won't have to carry here either.  See the sample below:

**EXAMPLES:**

```
      5830
      2967
       836
  + 38567
  ─────────
     30000
     15000
      3000
       180
        20
  ─────────
     40000
      8000
       100
       100
  ─────────
     48200
```

**Here** 80 + 20 = 100.  Using the old method of adding, the "1" would have to be carried.  Here we just add from left to right again to get rid of that problem.

**THE ANSWER!!**

## Lesson Plan #7 - Math (Middle School)

*"It is easier to resist at the beginning than at the end."–Leonardo da Vinci*

**TITLE:**  ROMAN NUMERALS

**SUMMARY:**  Roman numerals are no longer an essential component of math, but it needs to be considered as a part of our cultural advantage.  Students are fascinated by the "secret code" aspect of Roman numerals.  (Even certain street gangs have adopted the use of Roman numerals in describing what streets or area they are from.)  This lesson could also easily be integrated into a study of addition and subtraction, or world number systems.  Some copyright labels on books or videos still use Roman numerals as a mode of identification.

**GRADE LEVELS:**  6th through 8th.  Middle School

**GOAL:**  As a result of this activity, the students will know and be able to recognize Roman numerals as such whenever and wherever students see them.  They will also be able to:

1.  Identify each symbol and what it stands for in Arabic numbers:
    I - 1
    V - 5
    X - 10
    L - 50
    C - 100
    D - 500
    M - 100

2. Understand the source of each symbol.

3. Be able to transfer Roman numerals into Arabic numbers.

4. Be able to write the correct Roman numerals for Arabic numbers.

5. Have an appreciation for the historical value of Roman numerals: how they were used in the Roman Empire, and why they are no longer commonly used.

**RESOURCES & MATERIALS (BACKGROUND):**

Roman numerals were developed around 500 B.C. at least partially from primitive Greek alphabet symbols which were not incorporated into Latin. Using predominantly addition, they are read from left to right.

The symbol "I" for 1 was derived from one finger. Five fingers held up indicated five of whatever was being counted. The "V" then was the hand outstretched vertically with the space between the thumb and first finger forming the "V".

Originally the Greek letter "X", or "chi" meant 50, but in monument transcriptions, it is easy to trace the original symbol's change to "L", and "X" came to mean 10. Another theory for "X" is that the ten 1's were written in a row, and then crossed out with an "X" to simplify counting. Then the "X" alone became a shorthand version of 10. Yet another idea is that "V" looks like the top half of "X", as 5 is half of 10, and other scholars think that "V" doubled with an upside-down "V" meant 5 times 2, or "X". "C" indicating 100, came from the Latin word "centum", a hundred. (Also century, centennial, etc.) "M" is from "mille", a thousand. Larger numbers, like 5,000, are shown by putting a small bar called a "vinculum" above the "V" symbol, indicating multiplication by 1,000.

Until fairly recently a commonly used Roman numeral for 1,000 was "CI backwards C", derived from the Greek "phi", or "I" superimposed on "O". Half of this symbol, "I backwards C", led to "D" for 400, half of 1,000.

Generally, decoding Roman numerals is very straightforward. The largest numeral is at the left, with descending numerals moving to the right. Numbers are added as you go, as seen in these examples:

**CCLXVII** - 200 + 50 + 10 + 5 + 1 + 1 = 267

**MMMCCLXXXI** - 1000 + 1000 + 1000 + 100 + 100 + 50 + 10 + 10 + 10 + 1 = 3,281

**DCCXVII** - 500 + 100 + 100 + 10 + 5 + 1 + 1 = 717

*"If you don't have what you want, you are not committed to it 100%."–Anonymous*

Rather than continuing to add 1's to make 4 – "IIII" – or 9 – "VIIII" – subtraction was included in the computation of the numerals to simplify and shorten the resulting numbers. Therefore, 4 is shown "IV", or 5 minus 1. The smaller numeral BEFORE the larger one means subtract. "IX" is 9, or 10 minus 1. 40 is "XL", 50 minus 10; 90 is "XC", 100 minus 10; "CD" is 400, or 500 minus 100; and "CM" is 900, or 1000 minus 100. Students can follow the principles that subtraction takes place ONLY when the smaller numeral is before the larger one, and involves 4 and 9 in various place values.

Obviously, the cumbersome aspect of Roman numerals is one of the main reasons that they have been replaced by the Arabic system in our daily mathematical lives. Roman numerals remain important as part of the world's cultural past, and a unique way to express numbers.

**ACTIVITIES & PROCEDURES:**

**1.** Discuss the history of Roman numerals using charts, photos, pictures or whatever resources are available.

*"If you are not leaning, no one will ever let you down."–*
*Anonymous*

**2.** Have students make individual charts, showing each symbol and its equivalent in Arabic numbers.

**3.** Discuss the addition/subtraction aspects of the system, and have the students practice. Give each student 20-30 toothpicks, (the flat type), and form the Roman numerals for given Arabic numbers. For example, you might start with 106. have the students make this: ( CVI ), then have them change it to 206:( CCVI ), then 266: ( CCLXVI ), then 466: ( CDLXVI ),

**4.** Have students write Roman numerals of family members' birth years, or the number of students in the school, or other large numbers of interest to them.

**5.** Let each student bring in an example or picture of Roman numerals (book preface paging or chapter numbers, watch or clock, building erection date, statue or monument, outline topic numbers, etc.)

**6.** Read books, articles and encyclopedia entries about Roman numerals. Library skills could easily be incorporated.

Overall this will be an interesting cultural and historical as well as a study of the roots of modern mathematics expression.

## Lesson Plan #8 - Social Studies (Middle and High School)

**TITLE:** SEARCH & SEIZURE

**SUMMARY:**  One of the most engaging topics for students are their legal rights within a school setting.  The Supreme Court case New Jersey <u>vs</u>. T.L.O. is a perfect vehicle for a discussion of student rights, search and seizure issues and the "delicate balance" between individual freedoms and society's needs.

**GRADE LEVELS:**  7th through 12th.  Middle School and High School

**GOAL:**  The purpose of these activities are three-fold. A simple simulation engages students in a search and seizure activity that allows an exploration of students' rights within a school setting.  It also leads them into the issues of individual freedoms and society's needs.  Finally, it requires the investigation of search and seizure case law.

Students will be able to (orally or in writing):

1.  Compare how different people react to a situation.

2.  Explain why innocent people do have something to lose when searched.

3.  List the specific provisions within the Fourth Amendment.

4.  Identify school policy and student legal rights.

5.  Differentiate between student rights within a school setting and adult rights.

6.  List exceptions to the search warrant requirements.

7.  Explain how individual freedoms can conflict with society's needs.

**RESOURCES & MATERIALS:**  A copy of the Constitution.

**ACTIVITIES & PROCEDURES:**

Have the students imagine that you have taken the entire class to the library to do research on the Constitution.  The girls take their purses with them.  At the end of the class, one girl screams, "Someone took my wallet!"  The only person who could have taken it was in the class.

Break the class into six groups.  They are to answer questions posed to them as if they were:

**A.**  The guilty student
**B.**  An innocent boy

*If you stick your head in the sand, one thing is for sure, you'll get your ass kicked."– Anonymous*

C. An innocent girl
D. A girl with a controlled substance on her person
E. A with chewing tobacco and cigarettes (illegal in school)
F. The girl who lost the wallet

Pose the following questions for brainstorming and consensus:

A. Should a search of everyone occur? Explain.
B. Who should conduct the search, if one does take place? Does it make a difference?
C. Decide what you will do if a search of all is conducted.
D. Is the Constitution involved here? Explain.

When students are ready, have each group answer question A and then do the same for questions B-D. You should generate "I'm innocent and have nothing to fear." Explore that with the students. (Should law enforcement be allowed to search when or where they want because innocent people have nothing to fear? Wouldn't that cut down on crime?) You should also get the clever criminal who dumps the wallet and hides the money in a book. (How would the class feel having been subjected to a search that ultimately reveals nothing?) Ask the innocent girl or boy how they would feel if coincidentally they have similar denominations on them. Would they still be comfortable with a search? What about the students who possess illegal items? Should they get in trouble for what is discovered on them?

Finally, pursue the constitutional angle. What does the Constitution say? Should a search of everyone be conducted immediately? Does the Fourth Amendment apply to students? Do school officials need a warrant? Are they "police"? What would be the most efficient way to solve this? Is that the most just way? Raise the concept of individual freedoms conflicting with society's needs.

Students should now appreciate the constitutional provisions of the Fourth Amendment and how the Court can take the clear language and find exceptions of semantic expression.

*"The biggest risk in life is not risking."—Anonymous*

## Lesson Plan #9 - Social Studies (Middle and High School)

**TITLE:** POST-NUCLEAR WAR SURVIVAL

**SUMMARY:** This unit sets up a hypothetical dilemma and asks students to offer solutions based on their own reasoning and problem-solving skills. The unit begins with a scenario of nuclear war and requires students to make decisions which may affect the survival of humans on Earth.

**GRADE LEVELS:** 7th through 12th. Middle School and High School.

**GOAL:** The purpose of this lesson is to have students work together to reach a consensus of a controversial issue. It helps them to realize that sometimes there are no right or wrong answers—*only consequences.* After this lesson, students will be able to:

1. Evaluate various types of information and decide what traits and other factors are of most importance for long-term survival in an emergency or crisis situation.

2. Effectively present their opinions and arguments either orally or in writing.

**RESOURCES & MATERIALS:** No special materials are necessary.

**ACTIVITIES & PROCEDURES:**

Three days ago, nuclear war broke out around the world with massive attacks in all heavily populated areas. For the first 24 hours, radio broadcasts reported tremendous damage and loss of life in all areas, including the total annihilation of most of Earth's population. For the past 48 hours, there have been no broadcasts. Fortunately, the people listed below were able to reach a fallout shelter in time to take cover and survive the initial devastation. You must assume that those in the shelter are, as far as you know, the only survivors of the war.

Here is the dilemma: There are twelve people in the fallout shelter, but there is not enough food, water and other supplies to keep them all alive until the atmosphere is safe. To survive, the people must stay inside the fallout shelter for at least three months. The problem is that if all of them stay in the shelter, all of them will starve to death or dehydrate. There are supplies enough to allow seven of the twelve people to survive.

Your tasks is to list a description of each of the twelve persons, by age, sex, occupation, health and education level, and decide who will be allowed to stay and who will be asked to go outside (and probably die). The main philosophical question is, should some live and some die and why, or should all die together, why?)

*"Others can stop you temporarily, but only you can do it permanently."–Anonymous*

## The Magic of Tracing Paper and Colored Pencils

Whenever you go to a Science Class, History or Geography class, make sure that you take with you 300–400 sheets of tracing paper, obtainable from any art supply store and 15 boxes of colored pencils, obtainable from your neighborhood 99¢ store or any other dollar bargain type stores.  With colored pencils and tracing paper, you can easily create and instant and interesting lesson plan.  Let me give you an example.  Once I walked into a Health/Science class, and the subject was the human tooth, its parts and the various types of teeth of the human mouth.  What I did was have the class *trace* the colored illustration of the parts of the molar tooth that appeared in the text book in pencil, and with a ruler, draw a line to each part, such as the enamel, the pulp, the root, etc. and had them label each.  Then I had them to *color* the their illustration.  They *thoroughly* enjoyed this activity–*while* learning the anatomy of the tooth!  Tracing paper and colored pencils works wonders as well for tracing and coloring time lines in History, and who would not appreciate the Geography of South America better after having to trace the map and to color the countries, major rivers and major capitals of this continent.

*"What we Are is God's gift to us.  What we Become is our gift to God."–Robert Anthony*

## Emergency Lesson Plan on the Fly

Before closing this chapter, keep in mind that the most basic technique to handling any class that you walk into without lesson plans–*even your own*–is to quickly look around the class to find the most intelligent looking student and ask the following questions:

1. "Who is making an 'A' in this class?"

2. "Would you be my helper for this class?"

3. "What is text book that you use?"

4. "What is the last page where you left off?"

You then quickly scan the chapter and begin to teach from the last page where they left off and go forward.

Once last thing, it surely doesn't hurt to have a cell phone with you to quickly call the main office in case of emergencies or when sending a student out to get what you need is not the best idea.

*"Shoot for the moon, even if you miss, you will land among the stars."* –Les Brown

**CHAPTER**

# Secrets Of Self-Promotion

*"Success is when you do what you say you're going to do." –Emily Ruth Goins*

We come now to a revolutionary new way at looking at guaranteed self-employment as a substitute teacher. This is the concept of ongoing and pro-active self-promotion. One of the first things that you must adopt is a new attitude of who you are and what you are doing. Let me elucidate. You are not just a substitute teacher. You are a business and a service within yourself. You are the product (the substitute teacher), and you are the service (the service of subbing for teachers when they cannot go in). You are now to also see your potential teachers for whom you will serve not just as teachers but as you teachers/clients. And like any good business person, your job from now on will be to take care of your business by taking care of your customers, i.e., your teachers. Once you see yourself in this new light, everything that I will explain to you which follows will make perfect sense. And if you follow to the letter the advice and techniques that I will give you in this chapter, you will never, and I repeat, *never* be without daily work again, and you will be in only the choice schools which *you* have hand picked yourself. This is my promise to you.

## What If You Don't Self-Promote

Most people who take my courses and get my training materials on becoming a full-time professional substitute teacher are somewhat shocked to now have to see themselves as more than just educators, when they now have to see themselves as business persons, as sort of free agents who are bided for as football and baseball players who offer themselves to the best football or baseball team for the best contract. This is pretty much what you will now have to do as well if you plan to survive and thrive in this exciting profession.

But let us take a converse look at the same situation and ask the question: "What happens if you don't self-promote as a substitute teacher?" Good question. Now enter the world of the luck of the draw. What I mean by this is that you will be called upon by the computerized "Sub Finder." Let me explain. In most major metropolitan cities, after you have been processed to work for the school district where you have applied to, you are now placed into a pool of substitute teachers as part of a database of available teachers classified on the basis of what subjects you have stated you are willing to teach, whether you have chosen to teach elementary, middle and high school, and whether you have placed your availability to work for 1, 2, 3, 4 or 5 days a week. How you are placed on the call list is based on how you set yourself up in the sub system. First of all, you must decide if you want to teach elementary, middle or high school. Elementary level is of course where you find your "babies" in 1st, 2nd, 3rd, 4th and 5th grades, ages 6, 7, 8, 9 and 10 years old respectively. Your other choice is whether you want to teach in middle and high school which is comprised of 6th, 7th and 8th for middle school, ages 11, 12, and 13 years old respectively and 9th, 10th, 11th and 12th grades for high school, ages 14, 15, 16 and 17 years old. In many school districts you are forced to make a choice. Either you must choose to sub for elementary schools *or* middle-and-high schools. These are basically two choices. In this book, I cover only middle and high schools for two reasons, one: middle and high schools are my specialty and, two: there are many more middle and high schools in any relatively large metropolitan city which increases your chances for choosing the right school for you and for you to work everyday. So just by choosing middle and high schools as your specialty, you have already increased your chances for working everyday.

My final suggestion when initially relying on calls from the Sub Finder is to indicate during the application process with your district, that you are able to substitute teach for *all* subjects. I am very serious about this. Put down that you are willing to teach: English, History, Math, Social Science, Business, Computers, Science–*all subjects*. (The only subject that I personally won't teach is physical ed; I don't like the idea of getting dirty or sweaty, but you decide on this one.) You see, a good sub should be able to teach any subject *for a day*. Trust me on this one. Any good sub can teach any subject for a day. In most cases, a lesson plan has already been laid out and prepared for you, and you just have to see that the students do the lesson which their regular teacher

The next thing that I would suggest is that you put down that you are available to be called in 5 days a week. This will automatically place you higher on the priority scale in most school districts than were you to say that you are only available 2 or 3 days a week. Even if you only intend to work 3 days a week, my suggestion is to still place that you are available 5 days a week. You can always manage to be "not available" on any given day. The problem with specifying that you are only available, say, Monday, Wednesday and Friday is that if you are called in to work by a school that has gotten to know you on a Tuesday or a Thursday, you *can't* go in on those days specifically because you have placed down only Monday, Wednesday and Friday as the days that you will work. The logic behind this is that why should a person who has not made him or herself available to work 5 days a week be given the preference to work over someone who is there to help out every day of the week.

*"You will always find time for that which you love to do-no matter how 'busy' you are."–Charles Prosper*

has left for them.  As you learned in Lesson 5,  there are fool-proof techniques to handling any class whether you have lesson plans or not.  So before any self-promotion starts, you have to give yourself the best advantage for being called by the Sub Finder by:

1.  Selecting Middle and High Schools *preferably*

2.  Making Yourself Available for 5 Days a Week

3.  Putting Down that You Teach All Subjects

In the beginning, when you begin to get calls from the Sub Finder, you must prepare yourself to wake up every morning by 5:00 a.m.  The calls from Sub Finder begin at about 5:15 a.m.  The phone rings, and you hear this computerized job offer:

**Female Voice:** "Hello, this is the Sub Desk.  For the Los Angeles Unified School District *(Insert name of your school district here.)*  Please enter your employee number, and press #."

**Male Voice:** "<u>Reed Middle School</u>.  Has a job available.  You have been requested for this job.

**Female Voice:** "You will substitute for: <u>Ned Bant</u>.  The subject is: <u>Science</u>.  To accept, press 1.  To decline, press 2.

Now, at this point, depending on whether you accept or decline, the prompts will change.  Let's say that you press "decline" – prompt 2.  You will now here this:

**Female Voice:** "Please give the reason for declining this offer:  To select, <u>Iliness</u>, press 1.  To select, <u>Personal Necessity</u>, press 2.  To select <u>Prefer Another Assignment</u>, press 3.

You now press either 1, 2 or 3 to give the reason as to why you are not accepting the particular job offer you have been given.  I really don't understand why they ask you for the reason of your refusal because my experience has always been that within minutes if there is another job available, you will still get another call and another offer regardless as to the reason why you have refused.  The only way that you will get no more calls for that morning is to press * (star) when you hear, "If you would not like to receive any more calls during this calling period, press * (star) ."  Then and only then will the calls stop for that day.  To my knowledge and within my experience, the number of refusals do not

*"The best way to escape from any problem is to solve it."–Anonymous*

affect you during the regular school season. It appears, at least for the Los Angeles Unified School District for which all of my experience has come from, that only during summer months when the jobs offers come through Sub Finder when the jobs appear to be more scarce that you are penalized for turning down too many job offers. During the summer months, you may be taken out the Sub Finder system for an entire month and then be placed on an on-call basis if there are any leftover job openings. (Let me emphasize that the substitute teacher who practices the Prosper techniques of self-promotion can easily work everyday throughout all of the summer months without every having to rely on Sub Finder.) These secrets will be revealed to you by the time you finish this chapter.

The Sub Finder continues, but this time, let's say you press 1, *to accept*. You now here a different set of prompts:

<u>Male Voice</u>:   "You will substitute for: <u>Reed Middle School</u>. The subject is: <u>Science</u>. Please report to: <u>Reed Middle School</u>. Your job number is: 30878. Please report to <u>Reed Middle School</u>.

<u>Female Voice</u>:   "Thank you for using Sub Finder.

*"It is not how much you have but how much you enjoy that creates happiness."–Anonymous*

Let me give you a general tip. Always write down and bring in your job number. There was an occasion where I showed up for work, and I had forgotten to bring in my job number. The computers where down, and as a result, I was sent back home because the assignment could not be verified in my name. Also when you are going in to substitute as a result of a call from Sub Finder, and you find yourself running late, always call the school to let them know that you have accepted the offer and that you are on your way. I have also have had the misfortune in the early years of my career as a substitute teacher to have found myself running late, and instead of calling them in to let them know at the school, I just arrived. Five minutes before my arrival, the lady at the front office had called back into Sub Finder and made a re-request for another sub thinking that I had decided not to go in. Again, I was sent back home. Wasted day. No pay. I went to a movie.

In theory, Sub Finder would be fine, that is, to just let Sub Finder call you in every morning with a different job offer. The reality of this luck-of-the-draw approach is that on many, many days, you will be called in to sub for some of the most violent, disruptive and just plain bad schools in areas that resemble war zones by the infestation of the gangs in those areas, many students who will oftentimes be in your classes. If this were your only option, and if you have decided that you want to continue working as a substitute teacher, then you would just have to accept what you are given. But this is no really the case. You <u>do</u> have options. This book will give you the secret to unlock the doors to whatever school you choose to work in – in the *best* areas of your school district – and with the guarantee (from me) of your being able to work at that chosen school every school day that you choose.

### The Most Important People to Your Substitute Teaching Success

Before I go any further, let me let you know who are the most important people to your substitute teaching success. These people are:

1) The Ladies of the Front Office who Handle the Subs

2) The Teachers at the Schools where You Choose

These two groups form your customers, those whom you will serve, befriend and depend upon to give you work on a regular, daily basis. You will get to know and love them as they will get to know and love you. They need you as much as you need them. You entire philosophy of self-promotion will be based on always keeping this essential thought in the forefront of your and their minds at every moment of your working relationship. "They need you, and you need them." With this always in mind, let us begin the *Prosper Method of Self-Promotion for Substitute Teachers.*

*"To know which direction to take next, you must first accept where you now are."–Anonymous*

### Your Subbing Business Tools

Because the career of professional substitute teaching is every bit a business, you must first ask yourself, what are my basic business tools that I will need to operate this business. Your professional substitute business tools are varied, but the basic, essential ones are as follows:

1) business cards

2) cell phone

3) thank you notes

4) Andes chocolate mints

5) custom-made greeting cards

6) daily planner

7) digital camera

Some of the items on this list will appear obvious while others may appear to be questionable. *All* of the items on this list are essential and will *always* work with flawless efficacy when properly and faithfully executed.

## Phase I – Getting Your Business Cards Done

Let's get right down to the nitty-gritty as they say and get your business cards done professionally and the right way.  Since you are now in business for yourself (the business of promoting yourself and getting as many offers as possible), you must realize that you will have certain initial business start up costs and investments.  If I told you that by investing no more than $500.00 would guarantee that you would be able to work everyday as a substitute teacher and only in the schools where you choose to work for as long as you wish, would you consider this a worthwhile investment?  Unanimously when I ask this question in my in person training seminars, the answer is always a resounding *yes!*

Business cards done professionally will be your first investment.  When I say have them done professionally, I mean that if you are not yourself a graphic artist, then you must enlist the services of a competent graphic artist through your local yellow pages or print shop.  A good business card for your purposes as a self-promoting substitute teacher will have certain elements:

*"We don't see things as they are, we see them as we are."–Anaïs Nin*

1. Your Name

2. Your Title *(Substitute Teacher)*

3. Your Employee Number

4. A Scan of Your School District's Seal *(on the left)*

5. Your Color Photo *(head shot of your on the right)*

6. A Bulleted Lists of the Subjects that You Teach

7. Your Address (preferably a P.O. Box)

8. Your Phone and Fax Number

9. Your Email Address *(optional)*

10. A Short Slogan at Bottom *(e.g. "I Can Handle It!")*

Probably the best way for you to understand what this photo business card should look like is to give you an example of what my substitute teaching business cards look like.  Please see Figure 1.

**Charles Prosper**
*Substitute Teacher*

▸ Spanish
▸ English
▸ ESL
▸ Science
▸ History
▸ Computers

Employee # 314573

P.O. Box 29699
Los Angeles, CA
90029-0699
(323) 662-7841 *phone*
(323) 644-8221 *fax*

*"I Can Handle It!"*

**Figure 1**

*"I do not want to be happy. I want to be at peace, for only once I am at peace can I truly be happy."–Charles Prosper*

It is funny how some people worry about everything. I have had students ask me. "But, Charles, will the school districts object if you scan in their logo and use it on your card without their permission?" My answer is always that I would much rather ask for forgiveness than for permission. I have been using this card successfully for over 7 years. I have given it to countless teachers, principals, assistant principals, school counselors and administrators, and no one has ever mentioned anything to me about the use of the logo. Why wouldn't a school district want you to use their logo when it is properly associated with the job that you do for them?

My suggestion is to print up an initial 1000 business cards. You'd be surprised at how fast they get passed out in 6 months time. When you put your address on your card, I suggest that you use a P.O. Box instead of a street address. Sometimes, but not often, your cards fall into the hands of students. You really don't want too many students with your home address. This is the age of the cell phone. A cell phone preferably should be the phone that you use on your card. As soon as there is a vacancy for a teacher replacement, you want them to be able to call you immediately without looking any further. A fax number is good when a teacher or one of the front office ladies needs to fax you a lesson plan.

Now that you have your handsome photo business cards, you must observe and follow:

> Rule #1 - Always, always, always, always, always carry at least fifty or so business cards with you on your person, that is, in your pocket, wallet or purse. (Did I say "always"?)

From this point onward, everyone in the front office and all of the teachers whom you manage to meet or teach for will receive your card.

## Information Gathering

As you begin to know the front office ladies of the substitute division and the teachers of the schools where you want to work on a regular basis, will mark the beginning of the distribution of your business cards. As you do this, at the same time, you are entering in what can also be termed as the Information Gathering. As you are chatting and getting to know the front office and the key teachers whom you work for and those who begin to request you, you start to ask them key questions. These key questions are:

*"Worry is a mild form of momentary atheism."–Charles Prosper*

### Phase I - (Ask Key Questions):
- When are their birthdays?
- How many kids do they have?
- What are their kids' names?
- What are their kids' birthdays

### Phase II - (Write This Information Down Immediately):
- If you think that you will forget this information, have a note pad ready and write it down in front of them. If they ask you why you are noting down this information, just be honest and say that you don't want to forget when these dates arrive. That you think that it is important to remember and recognize the birthdays of your co-workers and their kids. Even before the days arrive, many will be touched by your gesture of *wanting* to remember. You will have manner to create some goodwill even before you have remembered to send a card or give a gift. You will be looked upon with good favor just for your genuine good *intentions!*

### Phase III - (Put These Dates Down on a Year-At-A-Glance Wall Calendar):
- To make sure that you don't forget, I suggest that you go to your nearest Office Depot® or Staples® stationery store, and purchase a *Year At-A-Glance* wall calendar on which you will write down all of the birthdates of your front office girls and their kids and the birthdates of all your key teachers for whom you work and who later request you on a regular basis. These birthdates and the key people with whom they are associated with are all their nice and visible in front of you at a glance for the whole year. Just by doing this on the path of your promotional process puts you immediately in the top 5% of substitutes.

**Phase IV - (When These Dates Come, _Act_ on Them!):**

- Keeping a careful record of these names and dates serves only one purpose and that purpose is to _act_ on them. When these dates arrive, give birthday cards and small thoughtful gifts to the front office workers and the teachers or, be it the case, to their kids. Your popularity will soar ten times and over as you begin to faithfully follow through on this.

Let me give you a little anecdote how I employed this creative thoughtfulness with one of my most favorite front office workers – Gloria. Gloria provides me with work as a sub _every_ day in the middle school that I go to on a daily basis which happens to be in a very nice neighborhood _and_ only 5 minutes from my home.

Gloria mentioned to me causally one day that her little son was going to make two years old upcoming in a couple of weeks. Now to give you a little background on my past experience, I used to own a party store, and I became very skilled in the art of balloon sculpting. What I decided to do was to create a 6 foot Rainbow Balloon Clown made out of air-inflated latex balloons. This was a singular spiral balloon column of rainbow colors: red, orange, yellow, green, blue and purple. I topped this balloon column with a large white balloon with balloon eyes, a nose and a mouth, on top of which I placed a red, blue and yellow conical felt clown hat. I told Gloria that I wanted to deliver a small gift for her son's birthday. She was delighted at the idea. She gave me her address and asked that I drop it over anytime after school. Well, the baby cooed with joy and excitement upon seeing what was coming through the door. He jumped up and down and screamed with happiness. Say I that mom saw me from that point onward as a very special person? Say I that offers to come in and sub became more and more frequent? What you give does not necessarily have to be a balloon sculpture nor do you have to personally deliver it. You can give any age-specific gift for your clients' (i.e. _front office girls' and your teachers')_ kids. The law of abundant life is simple: the more you give, the more you get. I am surprised that so many people still doubt this.

_"How often does a coincidence have to happen before God is given the credit?"–_
_Charles Prosper_

## Phase II – Using Your Business Cards Creatively

Now that you have your business cards ready and in your pockets, let's take a look at how to use them creatively to get the results that you want, that of getting more and more calls to your chosen school. I say chosen school, but I would like to point out that initially, you greatest effectiveness will result if you execute all of the promotional steps that you are learning in this chapter simultaneously with _two_ choice schools.

You immediately start to give out your business cards to the ladies at the front office, preferably *after* your first day of working at a new school. I suggest that you give them at least 25 cards or so. You make it very easy for them to pull out one of your cards and hand them to the next teacher who comes up to them and asks if they know of any available sub for a particular day that they will be out.

## Giving Out Business Cards in the Teachers' Cafeteria

You have just checked in with the front office to go in for a day of subbing at a new school where you haven't been before, but at a school where you would possibly like to go in again or maybe teach there on a regular daily basis. While other subs use their time in the teachers' cafeteria for eating and sitting alone, you know that this is prime time for self-promotion. First of all, always prepare and bring your own lunch to schools everyday. For one, you don't want to have to waste 5 to 10 minutes of your precious promotional time standing in long teacher cafeteria lines watching impatient teachers slide brown food trays across aluminum waste-level shelves as they make their way to the cashier. And for another, unless you are into grease, most school cafeteria food is really, really bad.

*"People don't change–they camouflage."–Charles Prosper*

You walk in to the cafeteria, and you look around for a table where there is a large gathering of what looks like regular teachers. Somehow, they are easily recognizable. They are these clique groups where they get together on a daily basis to bitch and complain about the school system, the brats that they have to teach, the principal, the union or whatever. You go over, and do your best to sit right in the middle of them at the same long table. As they talk and talk, sooner or later they will realize that you are not a regular of their group.

Someone asks you–"Are you a sub?"

You smile and answer, "Yes, I am." What subject do you teach?" you ask.

"History," he says.

"Would you be interested in knowing of an excellent History substitute teacher whenever you are in the need of one?" as you reach into your top pocket, pull out one of your photo business cards and begin to hand it over to him. You hesitate, notice that the other teachers at the table have stopped to listen to your conversation. Suddenly, you say, "Well, I don't want to deprive the rest of you." Then you proceed to pull out about a half dozen cards and summarily hand out cards to each one of them at the table.

Now, the question might come up in your mind. "What if no one notices me, or what if no one asks me if I am a sub initiating the conversation?" Well, again, you must become proactive and create the situation that you want to happen. The little technique that I am about to describe for you works well not only as an iniciator of conversation but also a great regular goodwill technique that you should execute *every* time you sit around a group of teachers in the cafeteria–even *after* you have become popular and after they have gotten to know you.

### Bring Out the Cookie Monster in Every Teacher

Do you know anyone who doesn't like cookies? I mean seriously. You may find someone diabetic or someone who has this weird anti-sugar campaign who is willing to ingest all of those carcinogenic artificial sweeteners and non-calorie, non-sugar sweeteners that cause diarrhea, stomach bloat and a host of other gastrointestestinal upsets, but show me the normal person who will resist the delight of one or two Famous Amos® chocolate chip cookies.

Every time you sit down to eat in the teachers' cafeteria, always go there with a box of cookies. Place the box on the table. Pick it up. Open it, and then offer everyone at your table–even if it means getting up and walking over a few chairs–a chocolate chip cookie. Let them each take as many as they wish–even if it means emptying your box of cookies. In the case where you are sitting at the table of teachers at a new school where no one has ever seen you before, someone is bound to ask you who you are, that is, if you are a sub there at that school. Even in the rare event that no one asks you who you are, you can still take control of the situation by introducing yourself.

"My name's Prosper. I am subbing here for the first time. I assume you are a regular teacher here," as you direct yourself to one of the nearest chocolate chip cookie teacher in front of you.

"Yes, I teach science."

"Would you be interested in knowing of an excellent science substitute teacher whenever in the future you may need one?"

"Why, sure."

You start to reach for your business card in your top pocket. You hesitate, look around at the other teachers observing your conversation as they continue to munch on the delicious chocolate chip cookies, crumbs falling on the corner of their mouths, that you have just passed out, and say. "Well, I don't want to deprive the rest of you. Here's my card for you too." You have out cards to everyone at the table.

The bell rings, and it is time for you to go to class. Self-promotion continues even as you walk over to class. You are looking for more opportunities to pass out your business cards into the hands of all of possible teachers who may call you in to sub for them.

### Ask for Directions–Then Pass Out a Business Card

Do you remember the story of Johnny Appleseed as he went across the country planting appleseeds wherever he could, and thus leaving the

*"If you think you're too small to make a difference, you haven't been in bed with a mosquito."–Anita Roddick*

growth of apple orchards on every path he crossed? Well, you too must become like Johnny Appleseed. The only difference is that your seeds are your business cards, and your orchards are your daily bookings at your two choice schools.

You are walking toward the building where you know your class will be. It is the red brick building off into the distance, just behind the flag that sits in the middle of the courtyard. As you walk up the stairs on the way to your room, you see a teacher standing in the doorway of her classroom. You pass in front of her, smile and say good morning. Almost passing her room, you turn back, and walk up to her.

"Hello, I'm Mr. Prosper. I am trying to find Room 323?

"It's just down two more doors on your right hand side. You see where that girl is going in with the red sweater?"

"Oh, yes, I do. Thank you so much."

"You're welcome."

You hesitate a moment before walking off and say. "What subject do you teach?"

"Social studies."

"Would you be interested in having an excellent social studies substitute teacher whenever you have to take off again?"

"Sure. Do you have a card?"

You go to your top pocket, take out two business cards and hand them to her.

"Hmmm. Nice business cards," she remarks.

"Thank you. Excuse me, and your name is...?

"Ms. Wilson."

"Well, nice to meet you, Ms. Wilson. I look forward to subbing for you one day soon."

"Sure, I'll keep you in mind the next time I'm out."

"Well, Ms. Wilson, you have a great day."

"You as well, Mr. Prosper."

"Thanks." You walk off and toward your classroom having perfectly executed a stage 1 technique of self-promotion which is that of greeting, meeting and passing out a business card to every teacher that you can.

At this point, you will also want to begin to make a record (in the notes area of your daily agenda—a subject I will cover in depth a little later) of the names, academic subjects and room numbers of the teachers that you meet. The purpose of this is that you must begin to memorize their names. Being able to recall the names of the key people that you meet is *extremely* important to your success as a self-promoter. There is an excellent book on the subject of memory that I highly recommend in the library of every serious public relations person such as yourself. The name of this book is. Hmmm. I trying to remember. Oh, yes. It's called *The Memory Book* by Harry Lorayne and Jerry Lucas.

*"Do not follow where the path may lead. Go instead where there is no path and leave a trail."–Jane Ellis Hopkins*

ISBN is 0-345-41002-5. The ISBN is the number that you would give your bookstore for them to quickly locate the book. This is a classic in the field of memory enhancement that has been around for over 31 years. This is must-reading! Your purpose for studying this book is to become a master at memorizing people's names.

You have made it to your class. Five periods later, the day is over. You think, "I might like to return to this school and teach again for this teacher." You are getting ready to leave, but you cannot leave until you perform another important ritual.

## Leaving Thank You Notes

When is the last time anyone has left you a thank you note for doing what was considered "just your job"? When was the last time *you* left a thank you note for someone for any reason which you felt grateful for or *should have felt grateful for?* Don't bother to answer me. I already know the answer–precious few and far between. That is all going to change now. Ironically, because so few people choose to be grateful and to show gratefulness with the gesture of a thank you note is what makes this technique so valuable. What makes anything valuable is the demand for that thing and its corresponding scarcity. Everyone wants appreciation and gratitude, but appreciation and gratitude is scarce, *ergo*, it is valuable. The value of gratitude and appreciation for you is that it will put you in a favorable light in the eyes of the teachers who you would like to call you first the next time they have to be out or to take off.

A few days before you came in to work at this school, you had already made a trip to your nearest stationery store and purchased a box of blank thank you notes. These are the type of horizontal thank you notes that are plain, have a simple embossed or gilded "Thank You" on the outside top. When you open it up, everything is blank. On the top inside flap, you tape or gluestick your photo business card. On the bottom inside flap, you right your message, something like:

> *Dear Ms. McCoy,*
>
> *Thank you for the opportunity to sub for you. I enjoyed your class, and I would love to sub for you again. Please call on me in the future.*
>
> *Sincerely,*
>
> *Mr. Prosper*

In the note that you write, don't forget to tape your business card to the blank upper inside flap of the card. In most cases, you would simply at this point, moisten the envelope of the thank you note, place the note inside the envelope, seal it, write the teacher's name on the outside of the

*"If there is no wind, row."*–
*Anonymous*

envelope, place it on top of her desk, and leave.  Not quite.  Wait!  There's more!  There is absolutely, positively the final touch the you <u>must</u> do!  Why?  Because *I* said so!  You must tape on top of the envelope, on top of your sealed thank you note–*an Andes chocolate mint.*  You know the type of mints that I am talking about.  Remember the last time you and your spouse stayed over at the Marriotte Hotel and when you came into your room late that night after dinner and dancing, you found that the maid service had come in and cleaned up your room–and left a couple of small, green, rectangular Andes chocolate mints on each of your pillows.  "What a nice touch," you thought.  And even though you have forgotten many of the other details of your trip, you still somehow remember that nice touch of the maid who left the Andes chocolate mints.  You see, what I am suggesting for you to do is what the hospitality department of the most successful hotel chains have known for years.  I am just asking you to apply some of the proven methods of public relations to *your* field of endeavor which happens to be working everyday as a professional substitute teacher.

 If you have any trouble finding Andes chocolate mints wholesale, you can order them online at:

<code>http://www.candyfavorites.com</code>

From now on, the minimum addendum to all of your thank you notes is an Andes chocolate mint taped to the top of your hand-addressed envelope.

 Now, think for a second, is there anyone else who should get a thank you note with their mint before you leave?  Yes, you are right!  The girls at the front office who are in charge of checking in and checking out the subs.  For this approach, I would suggest a little subtlety and surprise.  Sit down again, and prepare two more thank you notes: one for Elizabeth and one for Elsa.  Same procedure.  Envelopes addressed respectively to each of them, i.e, *To Elizabeth* and *To Elsa*.  Tape your business card to the inside top flap.  A written note on the inside bottom part.  Maybe something like:

> Dear Elizabeth,
>
> Thank you for your assistance in getting me to my class.  I would love to come in and sub for you again.  Please call on me in the future.
>
> Sincerely,
>
> Mr. Prosper

Insert card.  Seal the envelope, and tape your Andes mint on the top.
 As you are signing out, near their desk, discreetly place their notes and mints on top of their area, smile, and say goodbye.

*"All knowing is believing. Knowing is just believing that something is certain."*– Charles Prosper

If you recall, I said that minimally, you will leave a thank you note with your business card and an Andes chocolate mint, but there will come the time when we will have to take it up a notch.

## Restaurant Gift Certificates

This is a technique that you can start right out of the gate, or you can wait until you have taught once at a particular school where you would like to return, and then begin to add this to your thank you notes.

Elsa had called me in one morning a couple of days after I had left her that first thank you note. The assignment was to work an entire week for an English class. Everyday with the same kids at the same school. Nice. This is just where I wanted things to start going. My *thank you note/Andes mint* had produce the first positive result. "Now," I thought, "it is time to accelerate the goodwill process."

I went over to the Olive Garden®, one of the better family chain Italian restaurants here in Southern California.

"Do you have any gift coupons," I ask as I walk in and am greeted by the receptionist at the entrance.

"We most certainly do. You can purchase them for any amount that you want at the bar."

I walk over into the bar area, perch myself on top of one of the stool seats and wait for the bartender to wait on me.

"Hi, I'd like to purchase a forty dollar gift certificate."

"Sure," he replies.

"Here's my credit card."

"Here's your gift card, and it is good in any Olive Garden Italian restaurant." He smiles and hands me the my gift and credit card.

"Thank you." I leave.
I had no idea what Elsa's reaction would be, but I was excited in the anticipation of finding out.

It was the last day of my one week assignment. Again, I leave the mandatory thank you note and the Andes mint for the teacher for whom I subbed for that week. I now prepare Elsa's thank you note, with the business card attached on the inside top and the note on the bottom. But instead of just sealing the envelope and taping the Andes mint on the top as I would usually do – I inserted as well her $40 dollar Oliver Garden restaurant gift certificate for two inside of the card as well. My heart was pounding with excitement. I just knew something good was about to happen.

I walk downstairs to the front office. There she was sitting behind her desk answering a phone call. She hangs up the phone and notices me as I walk in.

"Hello, Mr. Prosper, how'd your assignment go with Ms. Romero?"

"Excellent, she has a very well-behaved class. At least that's the way

*"Everything has value. If you think 'nothing' has no value, then why do people fight over parking spaces?"–Charles Prosper*

they behaved for me all week."

I discreetly reach into the right coat pocket of my grey wool trench coat. She turns her head a moment. When she turns back, I say. "This is for you."

She smiles. Receives it, thinking maybe it's just another regular thank you note. She gently pulls the Andes mint off the top of the envelope where it is written "To Elsa" in my handwriting.

"Go ahead," I say. "Open it up. This one is a little different."

Her hand pulls out the thank you note, and out falls the Olive Garden gift certificate into her hands.

She leaps to her feet, throws her arms around me to give me a hug. Tears welling in her eyes from the joy of the surprise.

"Oh, thank you, *so* much, Mr. Prosper. You didn't have to do this!"

"My pleasure, Elsa. Maybe you might want to take out and treat mom one day to the Olive Garden. I'll see you later. I leave.

Phone rings the next morning. It's 6:00 a.m.

"Mr. Prosper, can you come in and cover for the next three days?" It was Gloria.

"I most certainly can. I'll be over in 30 minutes."

*"If you expect to be lucky, you will be lucky."–Anonymous-*

That next day, Elizabeth, the other front office worker gets the same Olive Garden gift certificate. Same excitement. Same response.

With the incredible success of this, I think, "How can I employ this technique with all of the teachers for whom I sub, particularly those would have the most organized and well-behaved classes."
There is a fast food chain of more affordable restaurants but with still good food called El Pollo Loco® *(Spanish for Crazy Chicken)*. The food is good and the meals are cheap. Broiled chicken, mashed potatoes, beans, tortilla and a Coke® for about $5.00 is a very good deal. Off to El Pollo Loco. I purchased ten $5.00 gift coupons. For the next ten teachers, each would get at the end of my assignment with them a:

- thank you note
- business card
- Andes mint
- El Pollo Loco $5.00 gift certificate

It is highly recommended that you always place the gift certificate inside of the sealed thank you note.

At this point, you should notice that the front desk girls and the teachers for whom you have been subbing are now calling you in more and more. (Keep in mind that you are simultaneously promoting yourself to *two chosen schools* using all of the aforementioned public relations techniques.) You should be into your second month of self-promotion. Because you are working practically everyday at your two schools the need to take calls from Sub Finder has diminished to almost nothing. No having to go out to bad schools in bad neighborhoods and spend most of your day in grief. You are becoming now a regular fact at your two schools. Teachers have gotten to know you, and the front desk has gotten to love you. Students also have gotten to know you and respect you. You notice that as more and more teachers call you in to sub for them, students also begin to behave differently and better with you. Things are moving along quite nicely. You are on your way to becoming a SuperSub.

As I am writing this, came to mind a book that I highly recommend for you that has been a classic since 1936 with over 15 million copies sold, and I think that anyone in the business of self-promotion, by law, should *have* to read this. It is called *How to Make Friends and Influence People* by Dale Carnegie. ISBN number is 0-671-02703-4. If at any time you had already read it, it is time now for you to re-read it and earnestly apply all of its principles. They work. Get this book, and reading it today!

## Promoting through the Teachers' In-Boxes

*"Peace is the pleasure of the soul."–Charles Prosper*

If you have been in a busy main office of any school in the morning as regular full-time teachers check in, you will immediately notice that after they sign in to begin their work day, the first thing that this do is to go over and check their in-boxes which is located against the wall. Each teacher has their own in-box. They look like open p.o. boxes made out of wood reminding you of those you would find at a post office which cover a wall from the bottom, midway to the top. Each teacher's name is written on a label beneath their box. In their boxes, they find bulletins from the administration for upcoming meetings, home room folders, new class rosters, mail, personal notes and whatnot. If you ever wanted to communicate something important to *every* teacher and all at once, via their in-boxes would be the way to do it. I am about to lead you to a very important promotional technique. You are about to engage in a promotional blitz and reach all of the teachers in your two chosen schools all at once telling them about you in a very positive way.

Remember how you utilized the services of your graphic artist to create for you your business card? Well, you will now solicit her services again to create for you custom made greeting cards. These greeting cards will go in every one of the teacher's in-boxes which could be as many as 150 to 200. If they usually arrive at 7:00 a.m., then you will arrive at 6:30 a.m. on this morning. Ask Elsa if it is okay if you put a greeting card in each of the boxes. Show her one of them. Chances are she will say yes. Each greeting card is in an envelope and addressed: *"To the Teachers of Kinley Middle School"*. Let me show you one of my successful greeting card promotions. Please take a look at Figure 2 next page.

**Figure 2** This is the front of the greeting card which says *"Thank You for Making Me Making #1".* There is a colorful blue, green and orange background depicting a seashore with bright orange letters.

*"Everything that has happened was meant to because if it wasn't meant to be, it would not have happened."–*
*Charles Prosper*

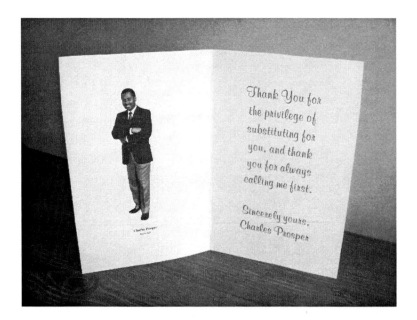

**Figure 3** This is the inside of the greeting card. On the left is a full color photo of me standing with my arms folded professionally dressed in a coat and tie. Under this photo is my name, Charles Prosper, and under my name is written *Substitute Teacher.* On the right is my printed message in a letter font which looks like handwriting. The message here is *"Thank You for the privilege of substituting for you, and thank you for always calling me first.   Sincerely yours, Charles Prosper"* .

**Figure 4** This is the back of the greeting card. At the very bottom, I placed a modified version of my business card without borders. The first line reads, Charles Prosper, the second line reads *Substitute Teacher,* and the third line reads Employee #314573. Below this information, front left to right, you see a bulleted list of the subjects that I teach. In the middle is the scanned in seal of the Los Angeles Unified School District, to the right is my p.o. box address, phone and fax information. The bottom line, in italicized quotation marks, I place a punchy quote or slogan. Here I placed, *"Have your students been 'Pros-perized' yet?"*

*"Perfectionism is a euphemism for fear, and procrastination are its fruits."–Charles Prosper*

Remember, whenever you do and design greeting cards to be placed in the in-boxes of all of the teachers at your two select schools, you should always place them in an envelope first and sealed them. Address the outside with something generic buy eye-catching like: "Attention: An Important Message to all Teachers".

## Employ Advertising Agencies

If you are really serious about your promotional process and if you are not afraid to *invest* in your *business*, then I would strongly suggest that you enlist the help of creative professional copywriters. Try to come up with more and more creative pieces. The promotional process *never* stops. You will execute a creative promotional piece for the in-boxes of the teachers at least once every two months. I feel like this. Just because Coca Cola® is number one, doesn't mean that they will stop advertising. They have to continually think of more a more creative ways for their message to *stay* in front of their customers. So it is with you and *your* customers. I create my own promotional pieces, and one of the most effective ones to date that I have done is the one which follows.

**Figure 5** This is the promotional that I did that consisted of three pieces: a red envelope with a labeled message *"Teachers! At Last! The Answer You've Been Looking For! (red letters first two lines) An amazing new secret guaranteed to relieve the stress of taking days off (black letters last two lines)"*, my business card, and a custom-made brochure printed on both sides which folded into three panels.

*"Remember always use a coversheet and engage in safe-fax."—Charles Prosper*

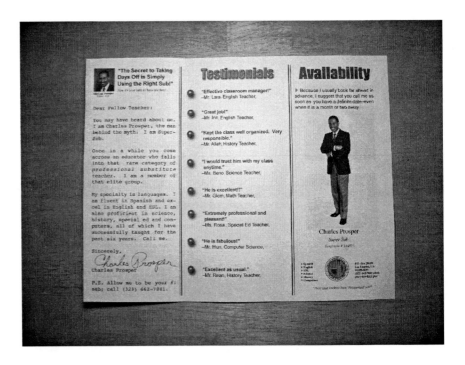

**Figure 6** This is the inside view when you open up the three panels.

**Figure 7** This is the front and inside flap open and spread out. The headline of the front panel is *"You Need Super-Sub!"*

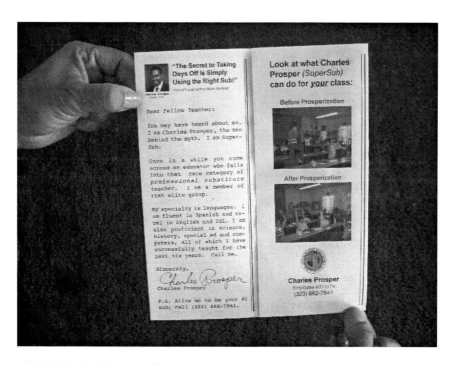

**Figure 8** This is what the teacher saw when they opened the first flap with the back outside flap folded into the inside.

To create this, I used real teacher testimonies, and students who posed for the photos. Take a close up look at each panel in the following pages.

THE SUPERSUB MANUAL •

*"A synonym is a word you use when you can't spell the other one."–Baltasar Gracian*

# You Need Super-Sub!

**Faster** than a 34-minute lunch break. More powerful than the final Friday bell at 3:19 p.m. Able to quiet noisy classrooms with a single raised eyebrow.

**Look!** Driving on the freeway! It's a bird. It's a plane. No, it's Super-Sub!

**Yes,** Super-Sub–a strange visitor from another school district who came to LAUSD with powers and abilities far beyond those of mortal substitute teachers.

**Super-Sub**–who can change the course of rowdy students, command rapt attention with his bare lesson plans, and who, disguised as **Charles Prosper**, mild-mannered certificated teacher for a great metropolitan school district, fights the never-ending battle for Quiet, Order and the Scholarly Way!

*Go to next page...*

**Figure 9** This is the front panel and the first image that they saw when they took the brochure out of the envelope.

**Charles Prosper**
Super Sub

## "The Secret to Taking Days Off is Simply Using the Right Sub!"

*Now it's your turn to have the best!*

Dear Fellow Teacher:

You may have heard about me. I am Charles Prosper, the man behind the myth. I am Super-Sub.

Once in a while you come across an educator who falls into that rare category of professional substitute teacher. I am a member of that elite group.

My specialty is languages. I am fluent in Spanish and excel in English and ESL. I am also proficient in science, history, special ed and computers, all of which I have successfully taught for the past six years. Call me.

Sincerely,

*Charles Prosper*

Charles Prosper

P.S. Allow me to be your #1 sub; call (323) 662-7841.

*"A professional is someone who can do his best work when he doesn't feel like it."–Alfred Alistair Cooke*

**Figure 10** This is the inside left panel, the introductory letter which tells of your qualifications in a person-to-person straightforward way.

*"The key to getting what you want is through __faithful expectancy__."–Charles Prosper*

# Look at what Charles Prosper *(SuperSub)* can do for _your_ class:

## Before Prosperization

## After Prosperization

## Charles Prosper
*Employee #314573*
(323) 662-7841

**Figure 11** When the brochure first opened up, the teacher saw the back panel folded inward showing itself to the right of the introductory letter. See Figure 8.

## Testimonials

"Effective classroom manager!"
–Mr. Lara, English Teacher,

"Great job!"
–Mr. Inn, English Teacher,

"Kept the class well organized. Very responsible."
–Mr. Allah, History Teacher,

"I would trust him with my class anytime."
–Ms. Beno, Science Teacher,

"He is excellent!!"
–Mr. Glom, Math Teacher,

"Extremely professional and pleasant!"
–Ms. Rosa, Special Ed Teacher,

"He is fabulous!"
–Mr. Hun, Computer Science,

"Excellent as usual."
–Mr. Rean, History Teacher,

*"A yawn is a silent scream."–*
*Gilbert Keith Chesterton*

**Figure 12** This is the mid-inner panel showing the Testimonials. See Figure 6.

# Availability

▶ Because I usually book far ahead in advance, I suggest that you call me as soon as you have a definite date—even when it is a month or two away.

## Charles Prosper

*Super Sub*

Employee # 314573

▶ Spanish
▶ English
▶ ESL
▶ Science
▶ History
▶ Computers

P.O. Box 29699
Los Angeles, CA
90029-0699
(323) 662-7841 *phone*
(323) 644-8221 *fax*

*"Have your students been 'Prosperized' yet?"*

**Figure 13** This the far-right panel showing my Availability and all of my contact information. See Figure 6 again.

Indeed, why are substitute teachers different from regular full-time teachers? There are many reasons why that the average person has not even begun to think about. Let us take a look at just a few of the distinctions of this special breed of teacher:

## Buy the Front Office Lunch

Who said school had to be boring! Now you are ready to electrify, Elsa, Elizabeth, the principal, the vice principal and every teacher who walks into that front office for whatever reason. Today, you will lavish with viands the whole front office with a lunch that no one will ever forget.

What I want you to do now is to look up in your telephone directory any type of caterers-on-wheels type of service. I want you to pick out the fanciest one that you can afford. Expect to invest maybe $150 to $200 for this one. You will treat the entire front office with hors d'oeuvres, fancy finger sandwiches, French pastry, sparking cider for beverage all decorated artistically with fresh fruit of all kinds. You request that this feast be *delivered* to the school. (Remember, you will have to do this twice as you have two primary schools that you are promoting to.) Ask your caterers to deliver it as early in the morning as possible, at least a couple of hours before the normal lunch bell. If they wear uniforms when they deliver, ask them to be sure to wear their uniforms on that day. You tell them to deliver it to Elizabeth or Elsa at the front desk, and to include a greeting card which you have purchased of the Thank You variety with a message, "To All the Staff at Rollins Middle School, Yours truly, Charles Prosper." That's it. That's all you need do. It would be a good idea to do this on a day that you will be at this particular school.

Now just imagine for a second what will happen immediately after the food is delivered. Excitement. Surprise. Joy. Smiles everywhere.

"Who brought in all of this food?" says a teacher with amazement as she walks in to the front office to pick up a folder from her in-box.

"It's from Mr. Prosper," replies Elizabeth.

"You mean that nice sub who I always see around here? The one who left those nice greeting cards for all of the teachers?"

"Yes, that's the one. He had this delivered for the teachers and everyone in the front office."

"You're kidding!"

"No, I'm serious."

"Could I get one of those finger sandwiches?"

"Help yourself."

"Do you have his business card. I misplaced it. I think I will need a sub for next week for two days."

*"If you are seeking creative ideas, go out walking. Angels whisper to a man when he goes for a walk"–Raymond Inmon*

On the day that you first employ the catering technique to the school, I guarantee that your name will echo through the mouths of all of the teachers and administrative staff for a long time to come. On the day that you have the food delivered, yours will be the only name spoken throughout the whole day, and you will receive a flood of requests to sub for that school. More requests that you will be able to handle. Trust me.

## The Digital Camera Technique

The technique that I am about to describe to you is the *coup de gras* for establishing your position as *the* number one sub in the two particular schools that you are promoting to. Do you have a digital camera? Well, you should. If you don't have one, go out and get one asap. You will need it for the next power-packed ploy that I will teach you.

You will need a digital camera of at least 5 megapixels and a suggested memory allocation of at least 512 megabytes. You will be able to take well over 250 photos with this type of camera. Though there are many great brands of digital cameras on the market nowadays, Canon® and Minolta® put out some very good digital cameras. (When shopping for digital cameras, make sure that it says 5 <u>megapixels</u> and *not* 5 *effective* megapixels. Whenever you see the word *effective* you are purchasing the *simulation* of camera clarity and not the real thing.) The neat thing about digital cameras is that as soon as you take the picture, you can see what it looks like on the tiny built-in LCD screen. If you like it, you keep it, if you don't, just erase it from the memory and take another. You then take your camera in to the many digital photo reproduction centers, and choose just the photos that you want without any waste of film and money as was done the old way will rolls of film.

Well, enough of the technique discussion of the specifications and niceness of the digital camera. "Why in the heck will I need a digital camera," you ask. Let's see how sharp you are let's see how long it takes you to guess where I'm going to take you with this before I tell you exactly what you will have to do.

Okay, you will choose a day when you take your digital camera to one of your two schools. On this day, you will approach every teacher that you see as well as your front office girls, Elizabeth and Elsa. You see Mr. Freeman standing outside the door of his history waiting for the students of his next period to arrive. You approach him with your digital camera in hand.

"Good morning, Mr. Freedman."

"Oh, hi, Mr. Prosper. How are you doing today?"

"Just fine." Pause. Mr. Freedman, I am making a scrap book and album of photos of all of my colleagues here, and I would be honored if you would give me the honor of taking a photo with you."

"Sure," he replies.

*"Never complain how heavy your groceries are."–Charles Prosper*

"Is that kid over there one of your students?" you ask.

"Rogelio, come over here a moment. We need you to take a picture of me and Mr. Prosper."

Rogelio comes over and takes a picture of you and Mr. Freedman in a smiling pose as you hug each other in an embrace of camaraderie.

"Thanks, Mr. Freedman, I appreciate it."

"Sure, you're welcome, Mr. Prosper."

Now, every teacher that you see who is not teaching class or extremely busy at the moment will be the object of your request for a photo with you. You will do this all day long. You will also go to the front office and get a photo with Elizabeth and one with Elsa. A good day would be to obtain at least a half dozen or more photos of as many people that you can. Do you know where I am going with this now? Still haven't guessed, eh?

Your next stop after you get off is to go over to your nearest digital photo developing center, and get two 5" x 6" photos developed of each teacher and staff person with whom you took a photo. Now, I think you are getting the idea. You will go in the next day and look for the same people who graced a photo with you, and you will give a copy to each. What do you think that they will do with this photo?

"Elisa, here's a copy for you of the photo that we took together a couple of days ago."

"For me! Oh, thanks, Mr. Prosper. *Can I put it under my glass of photos that I have on my desk?*"

Do you hear what she just asked you? *Can I put it under my glass of photos that I have on my desk?*" Let's take a real close look at that response. If you notice, it is a very common thing to see in many office type situations, people who work at behind desks all day oftentimes have a clear glass plate that sits on top of their desks under which you see a plethora of photos: of husbands, wives, children, pets, relatives and loved ones. For you to get placed under the photo glass alongside their family and friends is a very coveted position. Just think, there you are in an affectionate photo embracing Elsa and alongside of her "other loved ones" where she will look at a picture of you and her together, day after day after day. What sub is she unconsciously looking at *and* thinking about 5 days a week, 8 hours a day? You! You! You! When she hears of a vacancy, a teacher who needs a sub on any particular day, who do you think she is going to call first. You! You! You! With the other teachers who now have photos of you and them together, they will also place your photo with them under their desk glass and if not there, they will place them on theirs bulletin boards-or even just in their desk drawers. Whichever is the case, they will see you and think about you on a regular daily basis in a very positive and endearing way, and when they have to take off. Who do you think that they will call? You!

*"God is in control of randomness, and every coincidence happens for a reason."–* Charles Prosper

You! You!

## Carry a Teacher's ID Card Around Your Neck

Let me give you a way to solidify your image of belonging to the two schools where you teach. Three or four times a year, photographers arrive to take the photos for the student id's as well as the teacher id's. Most students keep their id's in their pockets, and teachers, whenever they use them, usually have them hanging from their necks by a cloth, belt-like strap which usually has some emblem or slogan printed on it like, "Our school is a great place to learn." At the end of this neck strap, there is usually a hook or clamp that allows you to attach the id to it which may or not be placed inside of a clear plastic sleeve. (These clear id plastic sleeves are great which you can pick up at any stationery store allow you to easily switch different teacher id cards as needed.) Please see Figure 14 below.

*"Luck is when preparedness meets opportunity."–Earl Nightingale*

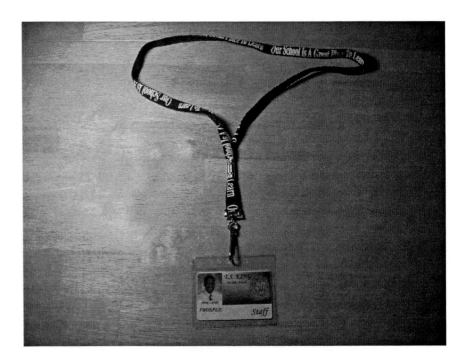

**Figure 14** This is a teacher's id tag which is worn around the neck.

Id tags are normally given to permanent regular teachers, but there is no law which says that a permanent regular substitute teacher can't get one as well. I have obtained several in the course of my substitute teaching career, and they are easier to obtain than you think. It just requires the desire to get one, a little planning and perfect timing to get yourself photographed on the day that they are taking id photos at either one of your schools. Usually, there is some type of bulletin that is handed out or placed in the teachers' in-boxes, or it may simply happen like this...

You are in homeroom which is the first period of the day where students gather for about 20 minutes to read silently and to listen to the announcements of the day over the intercom.

"Good morning, Purple Knights, this is Letty González, your student body president. Today there will be...and in the auditorium at lunch time, id photos will be taken for students and for teachers."

"Yes!" you think, "Now I can go and get my id photo.

The lines are very long at lunch time as students file up to get there photos taken. You stand behind the kid with the blue backpack. A seventh-grader sees you standing, and tells you that teachers don't have to wait, that they can go to the head of the line. Cool.

You walk up to where you see two adults standing near a large white photographic umbrella with a camera attached to it. They ask you to sign your name and subject on a card along with your grade level. Just put down the subject and the grade level you are teaching *on that day* (*Always* sign your first initial and your last name, e.g., C. Prosper. You don't want kids calling you by your first name.)

"Okay, Mr. Prosper, just sit on that stool just behind the white line. Tilt your chin up. That's it. Okay. Don't move." Click–Flash. "Your id should be ready in a couple of weeks." You thank them and head down to the main office.

"Hi, Elsa."

"Oh, hi, Mr. Prosper."

"Elsa, I want to ask a small favor of you. Since I am here practically everyday, I went over to the auditorium today to take my photo for my teacher's id card. They said that it should arrive in about two weeks. Would you leave a note for me in the Title One office that when it arrives to just give it to you to hold for me until you see me."

"Sure, not a problem."

Before your id card arrives, get a neck belt from the school and a clear plastic id card sleeve from your stationery store. When your id card arrives begin to wear it immediately and wear it everyday. Over the course of a very short period, when teachers, students and administration see you, they are subtly being given the subliminal message that *you* are a regular teacher in that you *belong* there at that school. Even though they know that you are a sub, they can't get it out of their minds that *you* belong there as *the* on staff resident sub for that school. When they think of a substitute teacher for that school, they automatically think of *you* first. If you have two primary schools then you must procure your id card to be worn around your neck from both schools.

## Get a Daily Planner

You are now at the stage teachers are approaching you as they see you on campus and are asking you if you are available to teach for them on such-and-such day. You must be able to take out your daily planner and

*"There are limitations to what you can control, but there are no limitations to what you can accept."*– Charles Prosper

check for your availability for any given day. Daily planners which can be purchased in any major stationery store is a spiraled book which you carry with you at all times. Daily planners contain the days you have committed to sub for your various teachers. You will also write down their names and phone numbers into the calendar on the day you will sub for them.

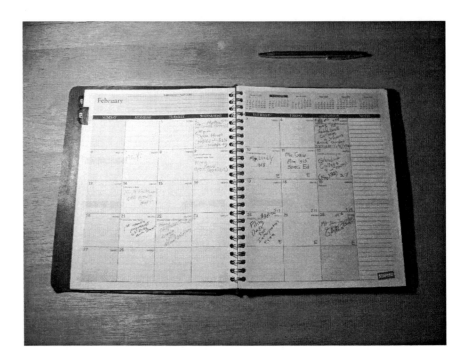

*"Acceptance = Peace."*–
*Charles Prosper*

**Figure 15** This is a daily planner.

It almost goes without saying that you must be organized with your bookings. You should be able to say at a moment's glance whom you are subbing for, at what school, what subject and on what day. Be sure to have the name address and phone numbers of your two select schools listed as well.

## Save Up 3 Months Reserves

This idea may take a little getting used to for many, for most teachers don't really think of themselves as in business for themselves or as entrepreneurs. As a full-time day-to-day sub, you are most definitely both a teacher and an entrepreneur. Since you do not depend upon anyone other than yourself for security, you learn very quickly that you must be prepared for the ups and downs of your business.

You are a freelance substitute teacher whose goal is to always fill out 5 days a week of work. Should on any given week you miss a day and work only 4 days a week – or if you are out a day or more because of some school holiday which you don't get paid for – you are covered financially by your reserves.

*"No one can really know if a situation is unlucky until it has played itself out."–Charles Prosper*

*"Shoot for the moon, even if you miss, you will land among the stars."* —Les Brown

# Secrets Of Classroom Control

I n the beginning of the book, I asked the question why become a substitute teacher, and then you were shown all of the reasons why you should become a sub if you are so inclined to do so: great pay, no lesson plans, no having to see parents, no grading tests, no creation of tests, not having to go to boring administrative meetings, full medical health and life insurance benefits, great schedule 7:30 a.m. to 3:15 p.m., Monday through Friday, and so-on-and-so-forth. However, with all of these wonderful benefits, you would think that there would be a mad rush to all of the various school districts by everyone who has a B.A. or B.S. degree. In spite of all of the wonderful advantages of being a substitute teacher, there is only one nasty, sticky disadvantage that would discourage the majority of would-be candidates, and that one disadvantage is the *discipline* problem.

The discipline problem in almost all public schools without exception is the bane of education. Discipline is such a problem because of the basic premise that the public school system adopt in today's educational climate. Bad students nowadays are never *expelled,* they or only <u>suspended</u>. I will never forget the day that I saw this 8th grader in middle school punch a kid in the nose and when the kid who was hit fell to the ground holding his face in pain was then repeatedly kicked in the head until he was rendered unconscious. The attacker was a problem kid who was always in trouble with the dean, was caught doing graffiti on the school walls and stubbornly refused to cooperate with his teachers and always managed to be disruptive, defiant and disrespectful.

When I saw this, I knew that this was the *coup de gras* for this kid, and that expulsion from the school would surely follow. Yeah right! He was given a one week *suspension!* A one week <u>suspension</u>? What this meant was that he got an administratively approved one week <u>vacation</u> from school, allowing him to rest and come back fresh and ready to cause more hell and havoc. I asked myself, "Why is that?" Why is it that bad students are never expelled, i.e., *kicked out* of a public school for any type of bad behavior. Well, the answer lies in the economic incentive to fill bodies in the seats. The schools need a certain level of attendance to justify governmental funds to keep the school running. This is why I have always said that administrators are very out of touch with the real world of teaching. Teachers hands are tied because

*"Life affords no higher pleasure than that of surmounting difficulties."—Samuel Johnson*

they can never do their best job of teaching because of the handicap of the administrative insistence in maintaining student bodies to the detriment of all concerned when certain student bodies should be expelled.

With that said, we must accept what is and make the best of it, that is, in spite of the situation of having in some way always having to deal with disruptive students who really don't want to learn on some level, let me show you guaranteed, sure-fire, foolproof techniques for vise-like classroom control. Classroom control is your ticket to a long, productive and enjoyable career as a substitute teacher.

## What Mr. Richards Taught Me

It was my first week as a substitute teacher. My assignment on this day was to sub for a computer class. I had come from an adult education background, and I had naively assumed that the same principles for teaching adults could be modified to teaching high school students as well. Well, was *I* in for a surprise!

I walk into a class of rowdy and talkative 9th graders.

"Good morning, class. My name is Mr. Prosper, and I am your sub for today." I turn write my name on the board. A ball of paper flies over my shoulder and hits the white board.

"Ladies and gentlemen, I don't think that this behavior is appropriate. I am sure that you know what to do during class when a sub is here," I say in a pleasant and affable tone.

"Yeah, free time!" someone shouts. Laughter bursts all over the room.

I wonder now if I got into the right profession. In spite of all of my polite pleas for order and quiet, they were summarily ignored. This was a very, very long 50 minutes. The bell rang. Everyone got up and rushed toward the door like a herd of wild rhinos. I felt dejected and disillusioned with this whole substitute teaching business.

I was on my one-hour conference break, so I decided to go out and take a walk down the hall when something suddenly caught my attention inside of Mr. Richards' class. He now had the *same* students that were just in my class, but there was an amazing difference. They were sitting in their seats reading and writing in total silence. No one even dared to look to the right or the left of them. They just keep diligently working and writing. I was dumbfounded! I was speechless. My jaw almost dropped to the floor. I walked into his class and asked him if I might observe. He nodded yes. Throughout the entire period was maintained the same level of quiet and order. The bell rang. The students did not move. Mr. Richards then calmly spoke.

"You may straighten your desk out and leave." Students quietly got up and walked out of the door in an orderly fashion, the last person gently closing the door behind her.

I almost got on my knees to *beg* Mr. Richards to tell me his se-

*"Gratitude is prayer."*–
*Charles Prosper*

cret.

"Mr. Richards, I had that exact same class, the *same* students, and they were totally disorderly and disrespectful. I walk here into *your* class, and they are model students! Totally well behaved and respectful! Mr. Richards, please tell me. How do you do it? My whole career as a teacher depends on knowing what you know about classroom control."

Mr. Richards looks up at me from his desk, pauses a moment, then smiles.

"Well, Prosper, I'll tell you. I don't care if they think I'm an asshole, as long as they do my work. I don't need to be their friend. In fact, I don't want to be their friend. I am their teacher. What the hell am I going to do with a 14-year-old friend! I don't want them to immediately get close to me. I want them to *earn* my friendship toward them by what they do for me. Then, maybe, just maybe we can talk and chat in a friendly manner."

When he said this, I got it! In a matter of a minute, I understood more about classroom control than I could have gotten in a one week seminar on theoretical classroom principles offered by the administrative class of the unified school districts. I've tried to think of a way to tersely and succinctly elucidate the philosophy of Mr. Richards, and I think I've got it. *"You must get in touch with your inner asshole."*

*"That old law about "an eye for an eye" leaves everybody blind."–Martin Luther King, Jr.*

## Nice Does Not Work

The first principle that you must understand to become a successful public school substitute teacher is that *nice does not work.* This is something that you will discover on your own very early in your substitute teaching career. You see, students love to have substitutes come in because they automatically assume that this will be a take-over-the-class day. I have had students verbally articulate to me that when a sub comes in that they expect to do what they want.

"With you, Mr. Prosper, we know that we can't get away with anything because you know how to control us, but when a regular sub comes in we try to get away with as much as we can," one student actually told me this in these exact words.

As soon as you walk down the halls toward the classroom of a new school where you haven't taught and where the students haven't gotten to know you yet as soon as they see you coming toward the class, you can hear the victory cry from one of the students as they joyfully give eachother hi-fives.

"We got a *sub!*" Translate, "We are going to have a good time today!"

When you walk into class, you will have approximately a 7 minute window to establish who you are and what you stand for in terms of discipline. You have to walk in there with a tough, mean-looking, no-nonsense, *we're-going-to-get-right-down-to-business* look on your face.

When I first walk into a new class where they have never seen me before, I don't even smile. I am not rude or impolite, but I keep that no-nonsense look on my face until I have them doing what I want them to be doing. My voice is terse, direct, strong and authoritative. Think of the kick-ass army drill sergeant. That's the image that I have of myself as I begin giving the instructions of the class. Sometimes, if they class seems fairly well-behaved, I will just begin by telling them what to do. I first write my name on the board, and then I begin.

"Everyone in their regulars seats, please. My name is Mr. Prosper. I have a seating chart here, and anyone who is not in their correct seat, I will automatically mark you absent." Suddenly you see them scurrying to their correct seats. (By the way, I say this whether I have the seating chart or not.) "Take out a sheet of paper. Go to page 203 in the green book, and begin to do the reading while I take roll." You must always have them start with something to do immediately. They only thing that students know to do with a vacuum is to misbehave and talk excessively.

The reason why "nice" does not work is because they see "nice" and the synonym for "easy to take over". After a first initial experience with me, I may have a student walk up to me and say this to me:

"Mister, you're mean!"

"Tell all your friends," I reply.

If I walk into a classroom and the class appears to be initially very disruptive and unfocused, I take a stronger approach.

"Excuse me! *Excuse me!,*" I bark out in a very angry tone of voice. "I don't know who you are used to having as a substitute when your regular teacher is out, but let me introduce myself, my name is Mr. Prosper, and I don't play around! In fact, if there is anyone here who doesn't want to be here or who thinks that they will have a problem doing what *I* say here today, let me know, and I will send you out to the dean right now! If you think that you can't handle being quiet, doing the lesson as I explain to you, *there's the door!*" I point to the door with one hand for emphasis.

Doing the first few minutes of the class, the students are regularly giving you tests to see if you will remain firm in your resolution to be in total control. Someone, takes out candy or food and begins to eat it in class.

"Throw the candy away," you command.

"Ms. Harris, always lets us eat in class."

"Do I look like Ms. Harris? Do I dress like Ms. Harris? Do we drive the same car? Do we comb our hair the same way? Is Ms. Harris here today? It is not about what Ms. Harris usually does, it is about what I say that counts. I'm driving the bus today. Anybody got a problem with that?" This is usually enough to establish your no-nonsense image right away.

*"The true object of all human life is play."*–G.K. Chesterton

### Leonardo DiCaprio in "Catch Me If You Can"

I don't know where it was, but it was somewhere I was reading when I can across the fascinating true story of Frank W. Abagnale, Jr.

Back in the 60's, Frank W. Abagnale, Jr. was an extraordinarily talented and brilliant young master of deception. All before his 21st birthday he successfully passed himself off as a pilot, a lawyer, a deputy district attorney and a doctor, just to name a few. It was one day I was in my local video rental store when my wife and daughter were out for the day when the dvd movie *Catch Me If You Can* starring Leonardo DiCaprio caught my eye sitting on the shelf. I picked it up, and read the blurb on the back...*inspired by the true story of Frank W. Abagnale, Jr.* "Hmmm," I thought. "This sounds like an interesting movie." Boy, was I in for a treat! You see, Frank W. Abagnale, Jr., had successfully impersonated many professions, and of course the most glamorous ones are always the first ones stated: doctor, pilot, lawyer, district attorney, etc., but what is not widely known is that his *first* impersonation, that which allowed him to discover his incredible genius was his impersonation of a *substitute teacher* on his first day at a new public school. When I saw how well he executed every major technique that I teach, it was uncanny! It was though he had time-traveled to the future, read all of my books and listened to all of my tapes, and returned to the day and the place where he was to utilized some of the finest classroom control techniques any master substitute teacher could ever use. When I first saw this scene in the movie, how he handles a rowdy class, I literally leaped to me feet in front of the television scene shouting "Yes! Yes! *Yes!* <u>That's</u> how you do it! Abagnale, you were a @#%* genius!"

Well, I don't want to deprive you of that scene of the movie. It went like this.

Frank W. Abagnale, Jr. drives up to the front of the new public high school with his mother where he must now attend. This is sort of different to what he is used to as he still has on his nice navy blue jacket with the former school's emblem near the lapel with a white shirt and tie underneath.

"You don't still need to wear the coat and tie, dear," says his mother as she turns to him, her hands on the steering wheel, ready to say goodbye.

"Well, I guess I'm kind of used to it." They say goodbye.

Frank is walking down the hallway inside a very crowed and busy public school. He sort of stands out like a sore thumb with his squeaky clean ivy league look amidst the roguish appearance of the other kids dressed in everyday plaid shirts, jeans and sweaters. He is holding a paper in his hand which obviously has the room number to where he is supposed to report.

"Do you know where 710 French is," he asks a petite-looking blonde student as she opens her locker to get her books out.

*"Nothing can bring you peace but yourself."–Ralph Waldo Emerson*

**91**

A mean-spirited big kid in a school jersey jacket maliciously and intentionally bumps into Abagnale, pushing him into the locker door of the girl who was about to give directions to room 710 French. The jerk in the jersey just chuckles at his mischief, and slaps his buddy's hand in a sort of victory gesture of his accomplished deed, a kid wearing black-rimmed, Clark Kent-looking eyeglasses walking behind him in a display acquiescent sycophancy.

Abagnale walks into a room of total chaos. Some students are standing on top of the desks clowning around. There is disorder and laughter, that type of disorder and laughter when students know that the regular teacher will not be there on that day. (What was amazing to me was that the behavior of public school kids has not changed very much over the last 40 years.) The bully in the school jersey also happens to be in this classroom as he and his buddy with the black-rimmed eyeglasses who was outside, both notice Abagnale as he walks in dressed more like a teacher than a public school kid.

"You selling encyclopedias?" cynically says the kid with the black-rimmed eyeglasses.

"Yeah, he looks like a substitute teacher," sneers the bully in the school jersey. Laughter and school mischief is heard in the background.

Suddenly, there is an intense, inspired and determined look on Abagnale's face. He walks toward the chalkboard, grabs a piece of chalk, and starts writing fiercely on the board. Eyes squinting to a no-nonsense scowl.

"M-r. A-b-a-g-n-a-l-e," he writes on the board in bold strokes. "Quiet down people!" he barks out in an authoritative command. Laughter in the back suddenly stops. "My name is Mr. _Abagnale!_ That's _Abagnale!_ Not Abagnahly! Not Abagnayly!" The ferociousness of his voice rises to a dictatorial crescendo. Students stop stunned in their tracks, standing with their mouths opened in disbelief, no sound coming out of them. "Would someone please tell me where you left off in your textbooks!" Silence. "Excuse me, people, if I need to ask again, I'm going to _write up the entire class!_" A cold chill of fear runs across the entire room. "Take-your-_seats!_" Abagnale barks out his command while pointing directly to the seats with the intensity of an army drill sergeant. Students scurry to their seats like frightened little cockroaches after the light has been turned on in the middle of the night.

"Chapter 7," says a one of the students in response to Abagnale's mandate to know where they left off.

"Would you please open your textbooks to chapter 8, and we'll get started." Abagnale walks toward the now subdued bully in the school jersey, the same one who pushed him on the outside against the open locker door. He approaches him from behind and surprise him.

"Excuse me. What's your name?"

"Brad," he replies nervously.

"Brad, why don't you get up here in front of the class here and read conversation number five?" Abagnale helps him up by grabbing him under his arm, and leads him to the front of the class. (This physical approach is probably not such a good idea in today's climate, but it obviously worked well in the 60's.)

The jerk in the jersey starts to read French passages very poorly from the French textbook as the other students laugh and giggle at his mistakes and poor pronunciation.

Now, the real sub enters the class. A timid, nervous-looking little old lady, dressed in a long brown wool overcoat which reaches her ankles, probably in her seventies, horned-rimmed glasses, thinning hair and too much lipstick stands in shock to see someone else teaching in her place.

"They sent for me. They said they needed a sub for Roberta. I came all the way from Dixon."

Abagnale, with one hand confidently in his pocket and the other hand holding up the teacher's French textbook, leans over with a smile and whispers to the little old lady. "Well, I always sub for Roberta." He turns back to the jerky kid who obviously paused to pay attention to his conversation with the other sub. "Excuse me! Why aren't you <u>reading</u>?"

"I'll never come back to Bellarmine-Jefferson again. You tell them not to call me. What do they think–it's easy for a woman my age and all the money it costs to travel. I tell you, they don't give a damn." Students laugh as she turns and walks out. How long would this little old lady have lasted in a class such as this? They would have emotionally toyed with her and torn her apart.

I don't care how busy you are right now. Yes, I know you are reading this book, but I want you to take this book with you, and go out to your nearest video rental store, and get a copy of the movie *Catch Me If You Can* with Leonardo DiCaprio, if for no other reason than to just see the scene where Abagnale transforms himself into a substitute teacher. That scene is sheer magnificence. Doesn't get any better than that.

In the next series of sections, I want to give you the discipline situations that I guarantee that you will encounter as a new or experienced substitute teacher. Some of these typical discipline situations are

- Restroom Requests
- The Class Clown
- Desk Tapping
- The Noisy Class

## Handling Restroom Requests

When a new sub comes before a group of students for the first time, I guarantee you that one of the most curious phenomenons that you will witness is the sudden need of multiple students to go to the restroom.

The bell has just rung, and you are arranging the lesson plans and beginning to take roll. The lesson plan is written on the board, and students begin to open their textbooks to write. Ten minutes into the class a student gets up out of her chair and walks toward you as you sit behind the teacher's desk.

"Uh, mister, may I go to the restroom?"
Now before I give you the correct response to this very common request as soon as substitutes arrive, how would handle this request? Would you say, yes? Would you say, no? And whatever you'd say, why?

This is how you'd handle it.

"Uh, mister, may I go to the restroom?"

"No, we just walked in. The class hasn't been going on even 15 minutes, and already you want to leave out? The answer is, no. Go take your seat."

"But, it's an emergency."

"I said, no."

She pauses a moment, as if to think, "now what do I say?"

"Uh...Uh," trying to look embarrassed as she leans over and speaks in low confidential tones, "it's a *girl's* problem."

"I said, no, go sit down and take your seat."

Wow, you are thinking right now, Prosper, how can you just uniformly say no to student who requests to go to the restroom. How do you know if it is *not* an emergency? That's an easy answer. Observation. Yes, observation. If after you say no, and the student just goes back and sits down with no more insistence, and goes back to causally doing whatever it was she was doing before she walked up to you, then in all likelihood, it was all a put-on and a lie. Let me put it to you like this. If you are a kid in middle or high school, and if you really, really need to use the restroom, and if you are about to have an accident just after a teacher has just told you no, and to go sit back in your seat, what is the most natural thing that you would do? You would walk back up and *ask again* – and this time with much more insistence and urgency in your voice!

"Mister, I *really* need to go. *Please!*"

When a the same student comes back up to me a second time, or if I observe them squirming and wiggling in their seats, I will let them go – but with a caveat!

"How long is this going to take you?"

"Maybe 5 minutes."

"Okay, if you take longer than that, every minute over, I will ask you to stay with me for that amount of time during your nutrition or lunch period. Okay?"

"Okay."

Zip. They fly out. Zip. They come back.

*"Most folks are about as happy as they make up their minds to be."–Abraham Lincoln*

## Handling the Class Clown

How do you handle the class clown? There is usually one in every classroom. To understand the mental dynamic behind the behavior of the class clown, you must look at the fact that he craves attention and wants to be in the spotlight. To cure him of his antics, you must *over-dose* him with what he is asking for. Let's take a look at how to handle the class clown. Let's go in class. I am giving a lesson on the marine life of whales to a group of 8th graders.

"Very good, class, we are going to talk about the marine life of whales. What is not understood by a lot of people is that whales are not fish but rather mammals making them closer to cats, dogs and even humans than they are to fish because they are warm versus cold blooded."

A hand goes up from this scrawny little kid sitting in the back with a mischievous grin on his face.

"Uh, Mr. Prosper, do whales fart?" The class bursts into giggles and laughter.

"Very cute. Now pay attention to what I am trying to explain."

The scrawny little kid hands goes up again. I acknowledge his hand with a suspicious nod of my head.

"Uh, Mr. Prosper, do whales do it doggy style?" he grins, trying to hold back himself from bursting into laughter. The class laughs again and thus distracting the entire focus of the lesson.

"Excuse me, what is your name?"

"Uh, Nicolas." His smile dissolves away into worried look on his face.

"Nicolas, it is very obvious that you need attention, and because I am a nice guy, I am going to give it to you." He has a horrified look on his face not knowing what to expect next. "Stand up." He slowly stands. "I want you to come up here to the front of the class and entertain us."

"Um, that's okay."

"Oh, no, it's too late for that. If you *don't* come up and entertain us now that you have interrupted the class twice, I will write you up and send you to the dean."

He slowly walks up to the front of the room like dead man walking just before an execution.

"Turn around, Nicolas, and face the class." Class is silent in anticipation with only few giggles piercing the air. "I'm going to give you five uninterrupted minutes to entertain us. Now, I am not in a good mood because you have interrupted my class twice, so you had better make me laugh. You have five uninterrupted minutes. Outside of destroying school property, you can do anything that you want. Now, go ahead and do something stupid."

Beads of nervous sweat begin to run down Nicolas' forehead as

*"Every second is of infinite value."*–Johann von Goethe

stands helplessly in front of the class not knowing what to do.

"Go for it, Nick. Do something," one the students in the class calls out to edge him on. Nick looks and me then the class in total silence.

"Now class, did I give him the opportunity to entertain us?"

"Yeeesss!" everyone says in chorus.

"Did I interrupt him at any point in giving him the chance to make us laugh?"

"Nooo!" they all chant with a giggle.

"Then I don't think that he should interrupt me anymore, do you?"

"Nooo!" they all say.

"Now, Nicolas, you go sit back down and be quiet. You lost your chance."

Now all of the class points their hands at him and laughs *at* him. Our class clown sits down chagrined and deflated with no more outbursts and wisecracks from him for the rest of the period.

## Desk Tapping

*"Some pursue happiness; others create it."–Anonymous*

A very nasty habit that student partake of themselves is that of desk tapping. What is desk tapping? This is simply a bored student's idea of entertainment by beating rap music or some other sound of jungle beat on the desk with their knuckles and the butt of their palms.

"Bump. Bump. Bu-Bum-Bump-Bump. *Bump. Bump. Bu-Bum-Bump-Bump.*"

"Excuse me, do you see me teaching class up here? Stop the tapping."

Silence. Then. "Bump. Bump. Bu-Bum-Bump-Bump."

"Stop the tapping. This is the second time I am asking you. Don't let it be a third time."

A little longer silence this time. Then. "Bump. Bump. Bu-Bum-Bump-Bump."

"That's number three!" you say in a no-nonsense tone. "Dayra, I want you to take this student to the dean." You write up a referral slip. (Something I will show you how to do later on in this chapter.) And hand the referral slip over to the person accompanying the offender. "Take this referral slip, Dayra, and hand it to the dean. Make sure you come right back. If he runs off, or tries to ditch. You just make sure that you hand this slip over to the dean. Somebody will round him up later on the campus if that happens."

The key thing with handling a repetitive behavior is give them a one, two, three count when the number three count means *out of the door.* When you send someone out of the class with a referral slip, select a trustworthy-looking person to go out with them. Let me tell you something else. When students realize that someone is about to be sent out of the room, you are going to get lots to volunteers to go out with them to the dean.

"I'll take him! I know where the dean's office is!" Hands shoot up enthusiastically in the air all over the place.

My policy is to always select the person who does *not* have his or her hand up in eagerness to leave out of the room to accompany someone to the dean. Anyone that excited about getting out of class is someone who is likely to *stay* out of class, roaming around the campus and getting into mischief. I always tell them, "Whenever, you volunteer to go, I always say, no." Always select the quiet kid who is doing the work as the one to do the accompanying to the dean.

## The Noisy Class - Standing Them Up!

There comes a time, especially in middle school, grades 6th, 7th and 8th that when you are trying to teach a class of students who absolutely no concept that it is a school and no a playground. They are some who are talking loudly, tapping on the desks, throwing paper, laughing, giggling and what not. It is as though you are standing up in the front of the class as an invisible person. You have got to get and keep their attention, and you have got to do it now.

"Alright. That's *it!*" you bark. "*Everyone.* Stand *up!* – *Now!*" you bellow in anger deep from the diaphragm almost shaking the walls. Everyone quiets down and stands so still until you can hear a paper clip drop. "Everybody! Pick up your books. I *said* pick-up-your-books – NOW!" as you slam the bottom of your closed fist on your desk. "I don't know who you are used to having as a sub, but my name is Mr. Prosper, and I don't play around in my classes. We will have this entire class standing up if necessary until you are quiet enough to sit down and act like students. You, young lady, pick up that book off your desk. I don't want any leaning in here. You will stand up straight with your book held in your hands. And if there is anyone who has a problem with that, there's the door." You point to the door. *(When you use the technique of saying, "If there is anyone who has a problem with that, there's the door," you never really gave anyone permission to leave. You simply said, "there's the door." Whatever the hell that means.)* You continue, "It's still not quiet enough. We will remain standing." It's gets a little quieter. You say, "It's *still* not quiet enough. It is not until I can here only the hum of the air conditioner that it is quiet enough for you to sit down." It now gets even quieter. "It is not quiet enough until I can barely hear you breathing." Even quieter. "Now, stop breathing," you say jokingly. Half the class inhales and holds their breath, cheeks puffed out turning red, they exhale with uncontrollably with a giggle. "Very well, ladies and gentlemen, you may sit down." Sighs of relief from having to stand are heard all of the room. "Now, don't make me have to stand you up again for we will then stand for the rest of the period.

*"If we can really understand the problem, the answer will come out of it, because the answer is not separate from the problem."–Jiddu Krishnamurti*

## Mrs. Harris and the Female Fallacy

Whenever I give one of my workshops on how to become a successful substitute teacher, and I begin to talk about the importance of strong character and forcefulness in dealing with middle and high school kids, they is sometimes the little demure lady who asks, "Well, Mr. Prosper, discipline is probably a little easier for you because you are a man." This is what I call the Female Fallacy. The people who ask this question have never met Mrs. Harris. You know, Mrs. Harris, don't you. We have all known a Mrs. Harris at some time or another in our lifetime as either a teacher, a parent or a relative. Well, let me tell you about the Mrs. Harris that I met at a school where I was teaching regularly.

I had heard so much about Mrs. Harris at this school. She had an incredible reputation for being a tough disciplinarian. The interesting part about her was that she was a very diminutive woman, probably no more than 5 feet tall and 100 lbs. soaking wet. But she had a personal presence that was no-nonsense and a voice that resonated strength that no one could deny the minute she walked into the room. I was on a break for an hour, and I had the opportunity to go in and observe her class and her technique first-hand. I walked in, smiled a greeting at her, and proceeded to go to the back of the room to watch.

*"No man is happy unless he believes he is."–Publilius Syrus*

Kids were walking in, and lollygagging about as they stood around their seats. Mrs. Harris became a little perturbed at the lack of organization of some of the entering students. She spoke.

"Sit *down!*" as her voice pierced the silence.

Everyone sat down...I sat down too!! She was scary.

The point that I am trying to illustrate is that gender has nothing to do with the ability to control a class. Be the teacher male or female, if you got it, you got it!

## Writing Up the Referral Slip

In every public school that you go to, there is a procedure for writing up and sending out the impossibly disruptive student out of the class. In fact, you should remember to always ask when you are first checking in the morning in to a new school, "What is your procedure for sending a disruptive student out of the class? Where would I send him, and what is the referral slip that you use, and where may I pick some up if I happen to need them?"

Though the referral slips may vary somewhat from school district to school district, there is a basic template for writing up a referral.

- Student is interfering with the teaching and learning process by...
- State what the offense is.
- 3 D's: Disruptive, Defiant and Disrespectful.
- Recommendation of punishment.
- Please do not return back to class.

**The Office Referral (Plain Example)**

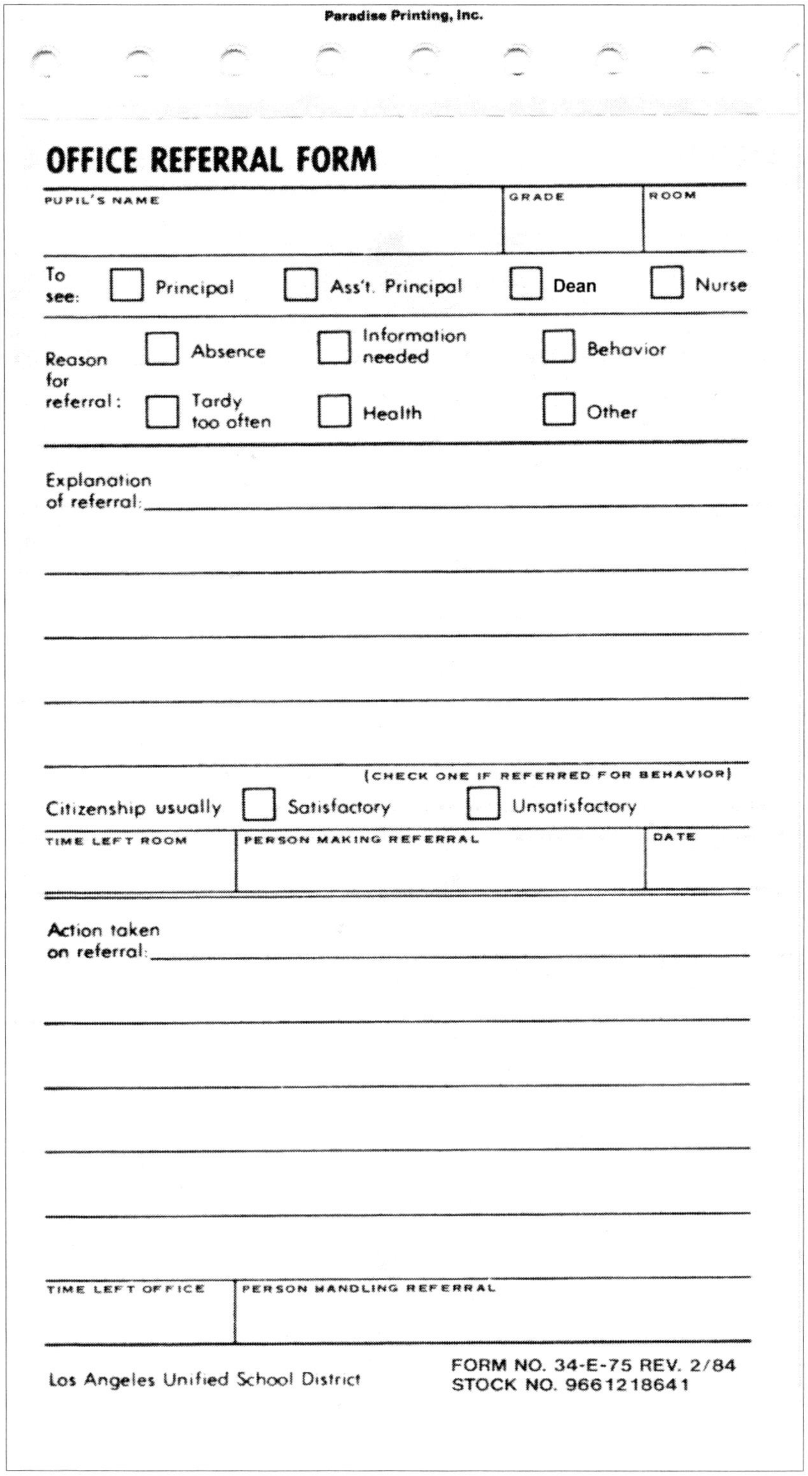

**Figure 16** This is what a standard unwritten referral slip looks like for the Los Angeles Unified School District.

## The Office Referral (Written Up Example)

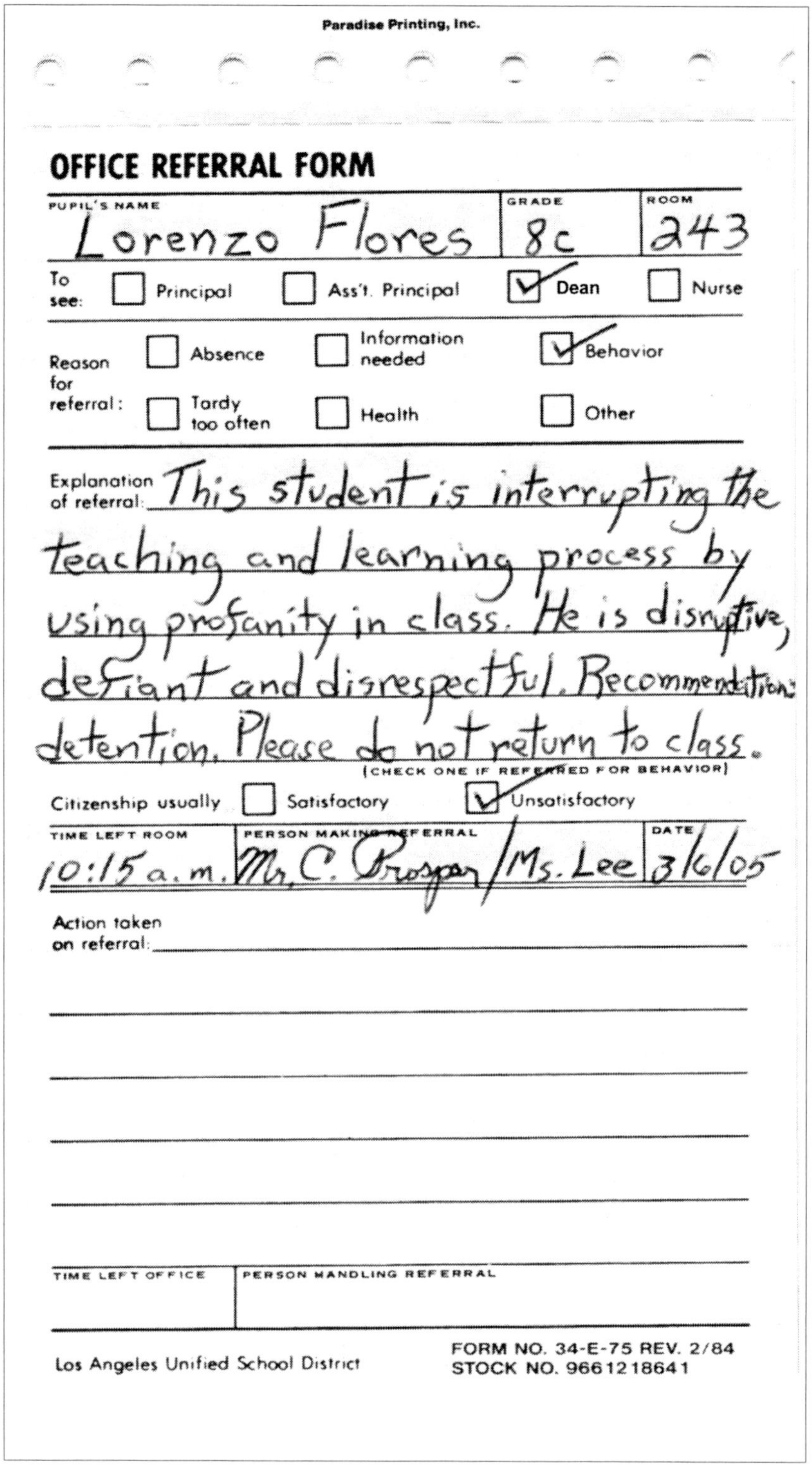

**OFFICE REFERRAL FORM**

Paradise Printing, Inc.

PUPIL'S NAME: Lorenzo Flores    GRADE: 8c    ROOM: 243

To see: ☐ Principal   ☐ Ass't. Principal   ☑ Dean   ☐ Nurse

Reason for referral: ☐ Absence   ☐ Information needed   ☑ Behavior   ☐ Tardy too often   ☐ Health   ☐ Other

Explanation of referral: This student is interrupting the teaching and learning process by using profanity in class. He is disruptive, defiant and disrespectful. Recommendation: detention. Please do not return to class.

(CHECK ONE IF REFERRED FOR BEHAVIOR)

Citizenship usually ☐ Satisfactory ☑ Unsatisfactory

TIME LEFT ROOM: 10:15 a.m.   PERSON MAKING REFERRAL: Mr. C. Prosper/Ms. Lee   DATE: 3/6/05

Action taken on referral: _____

TIME LEFT OFFICE    PERSON HANDLING REFERRAL

Los Angeles Unified School District    FORM NO. 34-E-75 REV. 2/84 STOCK NO. 9661218641

*"I long to accomplish a great and noble task, but it is my chief duty to accomplish small tasks as if they were great and noble."—Helen Keller*

**Figure 17** This is what a written up referral slip looks like. Notice in the block toward the bottom where it says PERSON MAKING REFERRAL, I first wrote my name, then I put a slash and also wrote down the name of the regular teacher.

## Presume Guilty Until Proven Innocent

Look let's face it. Bad students are not bad for a day; they are bad on a regular daily basis, and it is not likely that they will somehow become angelic because you, as a substitute teacher, walk into the room. In fact, in all likelihood, their behavior will be even *worse* because they feel that anything that they can get away with when their regular teacher is in, they should be able to get away with at least twice that much when a sub is there.

*"Common sense is instinct. Enough of it is genius."–*
*George Bernard Shaw*

You now know how to write up referral slips. You have an idea what they look like. One of the first things that you should do when you check in to work for a new teacher is to look in his or her teacher's in-box located on the wall with all of the memos for the day for past referral slips placed there by the dean. When you arrive to class early, you should also look in the teacher's desk drawer for copies of past referral slips that have been recently written out. The purpose of this detective work is to discover ahead of time who are the regular perpetrators of class misconduct and misbehavior. You can also get an idea what the classes are like for any particular teacher by how heavy a supply of referral slips are maintained in their drawers. If you can't find any, this could be a good sign. If you find a huge stack in each drawer, you're going to have a problem on your hands for certain periods. The key is to find out before they come in which periods tend to be the worst and who are the worst students. When you find a referral slip with a student's name written on it, make a note of the name, and read carefully what the offense was. If it was profanity, make a note of it. If it was defiance, make a note of it. Paper throwing. Excessive talking. Eating food. Gum chewing. Whatever. Make a note of it.

Next thing that you must check is the teacher's roll book and grades. The grades are a very accurate predictor of behavior tendencies. What you are looking for when you look at grades are the worst of the worst. Something like F U U. F U U in any subject means that that student has not only failed the class with an F, but also that the behavior was marked "U" (Unsatisfactory) and a "U" for (Work Habits). The probability is that if the F U U student is not amongst the recent past referral slips on the desk, I would be willing to bet that their names have appeared on referral slips and their butts have sat in the chairs of the dean's office more than a few times. When I find these predictors of bad behavior, I presume guilty until proven innocent, and then I do the obvious.

## Pre-Write Their Referral Slips

My next step is to take my list of offenders, and for each period, I *pre-write* their referral slips. Look, bad behavior is always generic. What are they usually doing? They are interfering with the teaching and learning process of the class by...blah, blah, blah. You know what the template looks like. You fill out everything except the time you send them out of the room, and the exact offense. (Leave a little space on your referral slip for the specifics.) It takes time to stop the class and write out referral slips. You are minimizing the interruption of the flow of your teaching. (By the way, even if you don't have any referral slips when you walk in early to prepare for your first period, it is still a good idea to get a few from your neighboring teacher in the room next to you.) With referral slips written up, you are armed and ready.

## Circumvent Bad Behavior Before It Happens

The bell rings, and they start pouring into the classroom. Tyrone Hicks, Luis Banta and Tracey Patterson are the three that have their pre-written referral slips waiting for them at the first drop of the bad behavior hat. You look around for a well-behaved student. She is the girl with the pink backpack reading the first chapter of the history lesson.

"Can I speak with you a moment?"

"Yes."

You take out your list. "Who is Tyrone, Luis and Tracey?"

She discreetly points them out, taking care that they don't notice that she is putting the finger on them.

"Tyrone. Luis. Tracey. Would you come up here to my desk, I need to speak with you."

"What we do?" Tyrone complains with a frown.

The three walk up to your desk with their backs to the rest of the class that you have begun the day's lesson by reading and writing something from the textbook.

In a discreet but serious tone, you begin. "Look, I going to be straight out with the three of you. I called you up here because either I see that you have recently been written up, or you have been sent to the dean. You know who's who, and who you are. I only want to be clear with you. I am a substitute teacher who doesn't play around. If any of you do anything today in this period to disturb my class, I will immediately send you out." You give them a very intense and piercing look as you slowly say to them while looking each in the eyes, "Is...that...*clear?*" They either nod or grunt a reticent "yes". "Okay, go and take your seats."

You poise yourself and ready the slips in the first drawer on the right. With the first disturbance that any of them cause, you send them out immediately to the dean. As always, whenever you send any student out of the room to the dean, make sure that they go out with a trustworthy student. For most purposes, sending out two or three students is about the most that you want to send out to the dean at any one time. You don't want to give the impression that your class is out of your control. In the cases where there are too many disturbing stu-

*"A man's life is what his thoughts make it."–Marcus Aurelius*

dents in a class, there is an alternative method for getting rid of a large group of trouble-makers in a class – even be they as many as 4, 5 or 6. To eliminate this many trouble-makers at any one time without attracting the negative attention of the dean's office, there is the following powerful and effective trouble-maker elimination technique.

## Enlisting Your Lieutenants

If you send 2 or 3 students out to the dean's office, that's fine. But what if you have a larger group of trouble makers? In this case, you need to enlist the help of your adjacent teachers in the rooms to the right, the left and in front of you. Let me explain. Regular teachers are very familiar with the discipline problems that other teachers have. It is <u>very</u> common in most schools for teachers to take, that is, hold a misbehaving student in their class thus isolating them from their usual environment thus causing the misbehaving student to feel disoriented and "out of place." Students as a rule do not like to be sent to another teacher's room for many reasons:

1. They are not around their friends.
2. They usually are placed in a boring corner where they either do their assignment alone or stare at the corner or the wall.
3. They are sometimes scolded or embarrassed in front of the other class by the teacher who receives them.

The most important reason for you to send them out is that *you* get rid of the problem regardless what happens to them or what they feel.

You can enlist as many cooperating teachers (lieutenants) as you have time to talk to before your period. This is the way that you do it. You first make note of who the misbehaving students are on a regular basis utilizing the techniques previously explained in the last section, that is, looking for copies of recent referral slips that have been written up as well as noticing the academic as well as the behavior grades. Write their names down on a special "guilty" list. Make a count of them, then go out before your period starts and enlist your lieutenants.

"Excuse me, my name is Mr. Prosper, and I am subbing for Mrs. McCoy's class today right across from you in room 243. There are a couple of students that have a reputation for disrupting the class. I was wondering, if I had to, if I could send one or two of them over to your class to isolate them and have them do their work over here?"

"Sure, send them over with another student and a note from you. I'll take care of them. I'll make them sorry that you sent them over."

"And you are...?"

"Mr. Meyers."

"Glad to meet you, Mr. Meyers. I appreciate your help. By the way, here is my business card in case you are ever in need of a good sub."

*"A hero is a man who does what he can do."–Romain Rolland*

Make your rounds in the same way with as many teachers that you need to enlist. Go on the second and third floors of the building if you need to find more available helping teachers. Once you have you completed list of teachers, you can go back to your room with the total confidence that if any disturbance occurs with any of the "presumed guilty", you will able to take care of the situation with no problem whatsoever.

## The Power of Seating Charts

One of the most effective methods for establishing control over students is to make them abide by the seating chart. The seating chart is one designated by the regular teacher where each student should be sitting. The tendency when you come in as a sub is that they tend to sit by their chat buddies and wherever they want which is a statement of their intentions to not have a regular organized day of teaching. You must do your best to find the teacher's seating chart, and explain as soon as they come in that they are to take their regular seats.

"Okay everyone. I want you to come in and take your regular seats. *Excuse* me! I need everyone's attention! I want to let you know how I do things when I come in to sub. I have a seating chart here, and if there is anyone who is not in his correct seat, I will automatically mark you absent." It's so funny. At this point, you will see many students scurrying across the room to go to their correct seats. The funny part about it is that I will *say* that I have the seating chart and that I will mark them absent if they are not in their proper seats when I take roll – *whether I have a seating chart or not!*

When the class starts, regardless of where their regular seat is, if you discover that there are any annoying chat groups that have emerged, it is your call to separate them and change the seating order.

"Excuse me. You two girls over there have been talking nonstoop for the last fifteen minutes. Let's see, Monica, I want you to come and sit up here next to me."

"But this is where I sit."

"Not today it's not."

"Ms. McCoy always lets me sit here. I'm not going to talk anymore. Please don't change me. I don't like it up there."

"Look, you are wasting my class time. Either you move up here, or I will send you out of class. Make your choice. Quickly. I don't have time to waste talking about where you want to sit. *Move it! Now!*"

## What About Cell Phones, CD Players, Food, Drink and Gum?

You will discover very early on in your career as a substitute teacher that students will try to get away with obviously prohibited items when you walk in to teach them for the first time. There are certain items that

*"You can have anything that you want; you just can't have everything that you want."–* Anonymous

most school districts will absolutely not tolerate, and it would be good to inform yourself on the letter of the law for that school district for what is and is not permitted. That notwithstanding, you must also become the law unto yourself as to what you will and will not accept in your class.

- **Cell Phones** – Most school districts have a written policy about not allowing cell phone to be used in the classroom. I never allow the use of cell phones in any of my classes, and I will threaten taking them and handing the phones over to the dean for them to pick it up later.

- **CD Players** – I never allow those things in my classes even if the student tells me, as I have heard to my amazement that some teachers let them listen to CD players to "help them relax" while reading. What a bunch of crock! CD players will do more to keep the student distracted from you and the lesson that any possible imagined relaxation benefit.

- **Food** – No food in class. That's what lunch and nutrition time is for. In addition to the hyperactivity produced by the eating of candy, which by the way some students consider "food", you will find yourself picking up Skittles, Hot Cheetos and all sorts of assorted candy wrappers at the back of the class.

- **Drink** – No drink, except maybe water if it is kept in a bottle and off of the desk.

- **Gum** – No gum. Not only will some students chew, smack and pop gum loudly in the class as you are teaching, what do you think they are going to do with gum when they are not interested in chewing it anymore. Yes, you guessed it. On the floor. Under the desk, and

*"If you run after two hares, you will catch neither."–* Thomas Fuller

sometimes on the seat. Have you ever stepped on gum after buying a new pair of shoes? Have you ever sat on a chair that had gum on it? Urge to kill? Yeah, a little. No gum.

"But Ms. Yang always let's us eat in class."

"Do I look like Ms. Yang? Do I dress like Ms. Yang? Do we comb our hair the same way? Drive the same car? Wear the same shoes? She is not here today. So it is what I say. Throw the food away–*now!*"

## Pepper Your Language

This next technique, I would say for you to use sparingly, and to use it preferably in middle school versus high school, middle school being 6th, 7th and 8th grades which corresponds to 11, 12 and 13 year olds. This "pepper your language" technique only works if you have the personality to pull it off. For little old ladies from the midwest who are thinking of going into substitute teaching as part of their semi-retirement, I have pull out the smelling salts for this one. Peppering your speech means to use "marginal" swear words. Here are some of *my* examples:

*"Do you prefer that you be right, or that you be happy?"–A Course In Miracles*

- "Don't *piss* me off !"

- "Hell no you can't go !"

- "I'm not a dumbass, okay ! So don't try to pull that with me."

Now if you don't have enough discernment to know what's marginal and what's not, I would suggest that you stay away from "peppered language". You don't want to sound like the speech that is bleeped off in the heated altercations of the Jerry Springer show.

## Get Physical (with Inanimate Objects)

You can't hit an irritating kid (as much as you might like to), but you *can* symbolically do the next best thing. Again, use this technique sparingly and preferably only in the middle school level. For very disruptive classes, I have had to use extreme attention-getters on occasions. Such as?:

- Slam on a table.

- Knock over a chair (an empty one please).

- Throw a board eraser or chalk on the floor.

These occasional *getting-physical-with-inanimate-objects* techniques works even more emphatically if you include peppered language along with it. Keep in mind that this is psychological warfare with the goal of total classroom control.

## Extreme Discipline Situations

Sometimes you will find yourself in a nightmare class. Students who are unusually unruly, profane, vulgar and defiant. If you feel that you are trying to handle a situation where either you are another student are in any danger of a physically aggressive student, then you must do what it takes in this case. There are times, though thankfully that do not happen often, when you will have to pick up your cell phone or the phone that is located on the wall in your classroom and do one of two things:

- Call the Campus Aide from the main office for someone to come in and assist you.

- Call the main office and request the campus police if that is available.

*"God's delays are not God's denials."–Robert Schuller*

My take, on having to execute extreme discipline, in any particular school on a regular basis is a clear indication for me that maybe I should think twice about going back to that school. Remember, as a substitute teacher, you are not bound to any school by contract. You have options, and you have the ability to choose.

## The Godfather Technique (Removing the Intractable Kid)

I came across this technique of classroom control rather by accident. Now before I explain to you how it works, let me emphasize that you may never need to use it during all of the years of your substitute teaching because the situation that evokes its need is very rare.

If you remember early on in the chapter, I explained to you how once students see that it is a sub that has arrived for that day, they will do whatever it takes to get out of class, particularly via excessive bathroom requests. One of the problems in letting too many suspicious students go out of class at the drop of the hat is that many will not go to the restroom as they have requested but rather will roam the hallways looking for another class where there is a substitute teacher so that they can walk in and pretend that they are in that class but have not been placed on the list yet. Most unsuspecting subs will just let them in. The purpose of the "restroom student" is to go around having fun by visiting as many classes where there are subs where he or she doesn't belong to pass an enjoyable time visiting all of their friends in the other classes. One day, I was on the receiving end of a student who just walked into my class interrupting it by going in to talk with his friend and then *refusing* to leave when asked! This was a very tenuous situation because when I called the main office to send someone over to take this student out, I was told that they were too busy and that I would just have to handle the situation myself.

"Excuse me! What do you think you are doing? You just walk into my class like nobody's business, sit down and start talking to one of your friends." I am just ignored. "*Excuse* me!! Did you hear me the first time? I want you to get up and get out of my class *now!*" He just turns his back to me in the seat and continues talking. The students giggle in disbelief. I couldn't just grab him by the neck and start choking him as much as I would like to. It was an impasse. In a situation such as this one, I do the only natural thing left to do. I pick up the school phone hanging on the back wall which connects to the main office. (I was ready to use my cell phone, just in case that the in-house school phone wasn't working.) "Hello, this is Mr. Prosper in room 266. I have a student here who just walked in from another class, totally interrupting mine and then is still here now and is stubbornly refusing to leave. He looks like a 7th grader. Can you send someone up to take him out of the room?"

"I understand your problem, Mr. Prosper, but the dean has his hands full right now, and we won't be able to send anyone up to help you. You will just have to handle it the best way that you can by yourself. I'm sorry."

"Okay, thank you." I hang up. I turn around and see the smirk look on this student's obstinate face as though to say, "You've lost, mister." In that exact moment, it was though God touched me on the top of my head giving me the words to say spontaneously just what needed to be said. I say, "Somebody. *Anybody.* Just get this guy out of here!" To my amazement, *half* of the class get up, run toward the student, lift him up and out the seat, carry him to the door and *throw* him out of the class! He flies out of the door, on his ass, sliding down the hall and spinning in a circle like a top. I was flabbergasted! I could just imagine some of the teachers' reactions passing by and witnessing this kid *fly* out of the room like an unwelcome intruder trying to crash a classy party.

"Wow! Who's the sub in *that* class?
"That's Prosper."
"Damn, he's *good!* Sign him up for *me!*"

## Educational Aikido

There is a type of oriental martial arts and self-defense developed in Japan called Aikido. Unlike karate and kung fu which consists of going against your opponent with strikes and kicks, aikido has no strikes or kicks at all. They don't even use the word opponent; they call them

*"If it's going to be, it's up to me."—Anonymous*

your "partner". Your opponent is called your *partner*. If Aikido doesn't use strikes or kicks, then what does this style of self-defense consists of? Non-resistance. Flow. Respecting where your "partner" wants to go. If your "partner" throws a punch in the direction of your face, you do not *resist* his movement, you *respect* and *aide* his movement. If his fist in punching toward you and is pointing toward the wall, you "help" him with his movement by grabbing his wrist and using his forward motion to "help" him to fly into the wall where obviously it is where he intended to go. In other words, you use the "partner's" force and momentum against him and in your favor. With that understanding, this is what I mean by "Educational Aikido". Sometimes a student is so bad and has a reputation with all of the administrators and the dean as incorrigible, it is sometimes best to go with his flow.

"Hey, Mister, I need to see my counselor about a problem I had." It is obvious that this student is making his best attempt to get out of class with an ostensibly legitimate excuse to get out of class. You have identified this student as being amongst the most disruptive in the school.

"So what do you need from me?"

"A pass to the counselor's office."

"What's your name?"

"Luis Navarro."

*"The prayer of the chicken hawk does not get him the chicken."–Swahili proverb*

"Here. Try not to get lost." He takes the pass and leaves out of the room. Don't those words sound sweet–*he leaves out of the room!*

## Miscellaneous Discipline Techniques

There are a couple of more discipline tips that I would like to give you before I close this chapter on discipline and classroom control. Sometimes when nothing else works, you can do this one:

- **Make them copy chapters directly from the book.** What this means is that if all else fails, have them copy word-for-word from the text book that is used for whatever subject you are teaching. Anybody who refuses to do what you say, just send them out to another teacher's class in isolation as previously explained.
- **Detain them 10 minutes when the final bell rings** The 6th period for whatever reason, appears to be the most rowdy when you sub as a rule. An easy remedy is to threaten them and follow through, if necessary, detaining them for 10 minutes (or more) after the final bells rings when they are all ready to go.

## Leave a Substitute Teacher Report

At the end of the day, it is advisable to leave a substitute teacher report for the regular teacher. It is good P.R., and it singles out the offenders.

## Substitute Teacher Report

Teacher: _____    Subject: _____
Substitute: _____    Date: _____
Employee# _____    Phone: _____

**Period 1**    What was covered:
_____
_____

Behavior Report:
_____
_____

**Period 2**    What was covered:
_____
_____

Behavior Report:
_____
_____

**Period 3**    What was covered:
_____
_____

Behavior Report:
_____
_____

**Period 4**    What was covered:
_____
_____

Behavior Report:
_____
_____

**Period 5**    What was covered:
_____
_____

Behavior Report:
_____
_____

**Period 6**    What was covered:
_____
_____

Behavior Report:
_____
_____

*"You've got to get to the stage in life where going-for-it is more important than winning or losing."–Arthur Ashe*

**Figure 18** This is a good example of what a SUBSTITUTE TEACHER REPORT looks like. You can type up something similar to this and make copies or simply write it up by hand on a piece of paper and leave it with the regular teacher.

## The Catch 22 of Public School Discipline

At the time of this writing, there are politicians who are proposing very out of touch concepts of school management. Until and unless schools are willing to *expel*, (notice my words). I said until school administrators, higher ups and paper pushers are willing to *expel* disruptive and pernicious students to those who want to learn, there will never be even a modicum of a chance to have real teaching take place in the class. Suspension is a joke, no more than a temporary rest for those students who don't want to be there in the first place. Though I loved him in *The Terminator,* California's famous governor, Arnold Schwarzenegger is proposing, in my opinion, a hare-brained legislation of teacher pay based on students' grades. If students make good grades, the teacher gets good pay. If the students make poor grades then the teacher is penalized by lesser pay. Even students who *want* to learn and when even taught by the best and most conscientious teachers on the planet, are limited by the time that teachers must spend dealing with those who are committed not to learn and are committed to see that no one else in the class will learn either.

The problem with *pay by merit* is that it is assumed that education is an *intrusion* rather than an *invitation*–that education is something that we can *stick in* or *force* inside of them rather than *e-ducate* which literally means to *evoke from within*. We as educators, are professional "door openers" not intellectual assailants of information against the will of a student.

Motivation to learn is a product of family values which starts at home and completes itself in school (if one is lucky). The problem with the public school system is in <u>forcing</u> a student to stay there when they stubbornly refuse to learn.

A student who <u>wants</u> to learn <u>will</u> learn even if their aptitudes are slightly less than most, but if a student refuses to learn even if they are at a genius IQ, will at best become a brilliant and clever violator of school rules and will fail *by choice* and not because of lack of intellectual ability or not having a good enough teacher.

By this system of paying teachers for students' performance, teachers are punished twice:

<u>Once</u> teachers are punished by having to deal with the conscientiously offensive students who literally cross their arms and say no to learning as well as who do their best to make sure that no one else learns by taking up the teacher's precious time by having to constantly stop and discipline <u>them</u>!

<u>Twice</u> teachers are punished by having their pay reduced because of the administration's <u>refusal</u> to expel these bad students so that the conscientious teachers <u>may</u> teach those who truly <u>want</u> to learn. Their refusal to expel is based on the economic incentive of needing bodies in the seats to the get the state funding to keep the school running ,i.e., running poorly.

Pay by merit would only make sense once all of the bad and disruptive students are <u>removed</u>, eliminated, eradicated, <u>expelled</u> or any other politically correct adverb that you would prefer. We must free teachers and that means free them to teach.

Whew! I just had to get that off my chest. Let's move on to the next chapter, one of my favorite subjects: *How to Dress for Success as a Sub.*

*"A genius is one who shoots at something no one else can see-and hits it."–Anonymous*

*"Shoot for the moon, even if you miss, you will land among the stars."* —Les Brown

**CHAPTER**

# How To Dress For Success As A Sub

O kay, let's get ready to rumble. I know that I am going to get a lot of resistance on this one because there is so much misconception and prejudice about dress. My contentions about what you should wear in order to get the greatest edge in standing out as a number one sub is based on the research conducted by John T. Molloy, America's number one scientific image consultant and clothing researcher. He is author of the phenomenal best-seller *Dress for Success,* ISBN 0-446-38552-2. You should get a copy of it. Everyone has an idea of what is good dress and bad dress. It is not until you can scientifically study the behavior of people either positive or negative in regards to certain colors, styles and forms of dress that one can make an informed decision as to what will help one get ahead in your profession, in your case as an educator and teacher.

## How Most Subs Dress

Only with a few exceptions, I have noticed that some of the best subs as for behavior control in the classroom and classroom teaching technique don't give a wit about how they look when they go in to work. I only think and imagine how much *more* effective they would be in the classroom and in improving their image in the eyes of the administration if they took a little more thought in their professional attire. (I might add that most regular teachers as well have a lackadaisical attitude about dress as well; it is a rare teacher nowadays in the public school system that understands the power and status symbol of the long sleeve shirt and the tie.)

As far as subs go, usually the worst dressed are those who come to work as though they are trying to emulate the attire of students. I have seen subs come to work with T-shirts, jeans, raggedy tennis shoes and backpacks. Backpacks! What the hell is *that* about? In this chapter, I will be accused of being ultraconservative about dress, to that I plead guilty for wittingly or unwittingly, conservative is what makes the greatest statement of your professionalism.

Some may claim that causal dress in the classroom is more a thing of comfort and the difference in casual dress and conservative dress in terms of advancing one's career or controlling the class is negligible. Well, I beg to differ. As a sub, you're trying to stand out in every positive way possible.

## Which School Professional Always Dresses Conservative?

I want you to consider something. You may see regular teachers and subs in all type of strange garb to go to school, and that, I insist is their prerogative. I have no problem with anybody dressing anyway that they wish to go to work. If the higher ups don't have anything to say about it, then why should I? But you are reading this book because you wanted to get *my* take on it. Let me go back to my original question of this section, "Which school professional always dresses conservatively?" If you haven't already guessed, it is always the principal and the vice principals. In the case of a male or female principle or vice principal, you will never see them come to work in jeans, T-shirt or tennis. You will *always* see him in a long-sleeve shirt and tie and her in conservative pants, dress blouse and maybe a jacket. Why? The answer is that conservative dress always conveys <u>authority</u>. And what is the definition of authority. Let's see what Webster has to say about it:

> **au•thor•ity\** *n, pl* **-ties**  power to influence thought or behavior

There you have it, authority, the power to influence thought or behavior. What else other than this are you doing on a daily basis if not attempting to influence the thought and behavior of students and the thought and behavior of the front desk and the school staff?

Whatever your partisan politics are, who is the most powerful leader in the world? The president of the United States. When was the last time that you saw the president of the United States, be he democrat or republican, give his state of the nation address on national television in anything other than a power suit, shirt and tie neatly wrapped around his neck? This is no capricious coincidence. The president is surrounded by some of the smartest people in the world who show him how to create his most influential image.

Who else's job is that of influencing the thought and behavior of others. Lawyers. How would you like for your lawyer defending your case come into the courtroom dressed like the average school teacher in T-shirt, jeans and tennis? Why would this offend you if he did come into the courtroom like this? Because intuitively we all know that when influencing thought and behavior is a life or death situation, we will always go conservative. Criminal lawyers will even have their convicted murderers and rapists come to court dressed in a suit and tie. At this point, we clearly know why.

So if you truly care about creating the most favorably image possible to enhance your substitute teaching career, let me give you some visual examples.

*"Forgiveness is the fragrance that the violet leaves on the heel that crushes it."–Mark Twain*

**Figure 19** This is a good example of how a professional substitute teacher should dress when he goes in to sub. Notice the long-sleeve light blue cotton blend dress shirt, maroon silk tie, navy blue 100% wool slacks and shiny all-leather black shoes (gold Cross pen in the upper left shirt pocket optional).

*"Faith sees the invisible believes the incredible and receives the impossible."–*
Anonymous

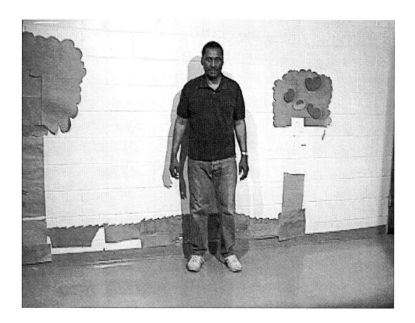

**Figure 20** Can you see the difference in effectiveness, or is it just me? This is an example how the great majority of substitute teachers go in to work. This is my example of how you should _not_ go in to sub.

After taking a look at the do's and don't of male dress, let's take a look at effective and not as effective ways a female sub may dress.

**Figure 21** Here is a simple example of good female dress for subbing. Notice the sleeveless gold blouse, black dress pants and leather shoes, with a leather black leather purse hanging from the shoulder.

*"No matter how big and tough a problem may be, get rid of confusion by taking one little step towards a solution. Do something. Then try again. At the worst, so long as you don't do it the same way twice, you will eventually use up all the wrong ways of doing it, and thus the next try will be the right one."–George F. Nordenholt*

**Figure 22** Though there is nothing intrinsically wrong with this outfit, it is much less effective than the authoritative look of Figure 21. The casual slacks and tennis weaken the image that we are trying to create of authority and professionalism.

## General Rules of Dress for Substitute Teachers

Stay away from jeans and casual clothes as much as possible. You may resist this one on me, but the idea is to stand out in a positive way.

**Guys**  – Long sleeve neatly ironed shirt, tie and dress slacks.

**Ladies** – Dress like you would were you to be interviewed for the position of assistant principal. Dress slacks or skirt, a neat blouse and impeccable shoes. Coiffure you hair tastefully, and use makeup sparingly; a little lipstick is fine.

*"Deep faith eliminates fear."–Lech Walesa*

*"Shoot for the moon, even if you miss, you will land among the stars."* —Les Brown

# Three Super Subs Interviewed

I don't want you to feel that by the fact that I work everyday in the choice schools of my district as a sub, that I am some strange anomaly of substitute teaching. There are in fact many super substitute teachers walking around, working everyday and working at pretty much the same schools on a regular basis, and none of these teachers knew anything about Charles Prosper before they achieved their super sub status. In this chapter, I would like the pleasure of introducing you and allowing you to go into their thought process by means of a personal interview that I have conducted with each of them to discover *their* secrets of substitute teaching. I would like to present to you Mark Bowerbank, mid-thirties, Louie Alcaraz, mid-twenties and Art Resendez, mid-thirties, three of Los Angeles County's premier substitute teachers.

## Mark Bowerbank (Super Sub)

**Q:** Mr. Bowerbank, basically, I want to ask you. Why are you a sub? Give me you your reasons. Why did you become a sub, and why did you become a sub?

**M.B.** Well, the reason why I became as a sub is before I wanted to accept a permanent position with LAUSD. I wanted to be able to see as many classrooms as I could as go to as many schools as I could before I picked, you know, one permanent position.

**Q:** Well, now that you have picked a permanent position as a sub, what is it that you see that appeals to you to in continuing to work as a substitute teacher at this time?

**M.B.** Well, the appeal is that again, you continue to see different classrooms. You can see different age groups of the students. You can see different subject areas, different school sites, and you kind of can get a feel of the dynamics of sort of different areas, regions, populations, you know...

**Q:** Now, another question, why would anybody want to become a substitute teacher?

**M.B.** I believe that when you become a substitute teacher before you accept a permanent position, being a substitute is one of the most grueling jobs, *(laughter),* out there, and I think once you become a substitute, you are sort of under the furnace, and if you could withstand the furnace, if you can get the worst of the worst, you'll be able to go into any situation.

**Q:** Well now, I have had people to ask me, that they want to become a substitute teacher. What is your advice for someone who wants to become a substitute teacher? What is your general philosophy of being a substitute teacher?

**M.B.** I definitely recommend becoming a substitute teacher. I think that when you become a substitute teacher, it not only teaches you about the students or the school and the classroom that you are teaching, but again it teaches you about yourself, and sort of your limits, your strengths, your weaknesses, and then you get to build on those, once you find those out.

**Q:** Do you enjoy working as a substitute teacher?

**M.B.** Yes, I do.

*"Feeling is believing."–Anonymous*

**Q:** What is the most enjoyable aspect about it that you find?

**M.B.** I like the flexibility. I like the different environments, the different types of students. I like the diversity. Yeah, and if you don't like a classroom or if you don't like a subject area, you can always switch.

**Q:** Are you happy with how you are paid?

**M.B.** Yes, I am. In some of the more challenging sites, I believe we should probably get more. *(Laughter)*

**Q:** This is for the perspective person who is thinking about becoming a substitute teacher. How would one as a new substitute teacher prepare for a day of school if they've never gone to substitute teach before or if they've never gone to a particular school? How would they prepare for a day of school? What is your advice?

**M.B.** Well, definitely get plenty of rest. You should be wide awake, and also prepare backup lesson plans if a teacher does not have a lesson plan. Prepare brief activities, ten minute, fifteen minute activities that you can use with the kids in case there is some extra time left over in the classroom. An educational video is also good, essay questions...

**Q:** Now, is this video something that you would bring, or you would look in the library?

**M.B.**   I would bring these things.  In case you don't have access to the library or in case you are in the classroom...

**Q:** So it's something like emergency lesson plans?

**M.B.**   Yes.  I always have backup worksheets or activities I can use in the classroom.

**Q:** Now, I want to get a general perspective.  What do you see different in approach in teaching middle school versus high school?  Can you tell me if there is any difference that you perceive or see?

**M.B.**   Well, definitely I think in middle school there's a lot more sort of catering or babying, I think.  I think in high school there is definitely more of a distance that you have between teachers and students, and I think it's because they want to be given the work and not necessarily prying into their lives, or, you know, figuring out personal problems...

**Q:** In middle school versus high school what is the philosophical or technical, or technique of discipline of middle school versus high school?  Can you comment on that?

**M.B.**   Hmmm.  Well, middle school I think you have to get to sort of the basics of telling the truth, not lying, honesty whereas in high school some of those things are a lot more foundational.  You might just have to reinforce them.  A lot of basic parental skills, you may be using in junior high school, whereas in high school a lot of that stuff needs to be sort of reinforced or a reminder.

**Q:** Like Shakespeare said "to be or not to be", the question is to shout or not to shout.  What is your feeling about that?

**M.B.**   I initially do not shout when I start off.  But, if I need to raise my voice, I will.

**Q:** Would that apply equally to middle as to high school?

**M.B.**   Yes.

**Q:** Now, we're going to go into some discipline concepts.  Does "nice" work?

**M.B.**   Does "nice" work?

**Q:** Yeah, being a nice guy?

**M.B.**   Intially, no, unfortunately *(laughter)*.  I think  when you  start

*"Man makes holy what he believes, as he makes beautiful what he loves."–Ernest Renan*

out you have to be firm. And you have to be strict, and I think that as time goes, you can sort of let up. But they need to know the foundation and the structure, and what they cannot get away with. They have to follow the school rules and policies.

**Q:** Well , let me give you some situations. This are typical that we all go through in the situation of becoming a substitute teacher. Here are three situations, and tell me if it is three answers or one answer? The classroom clown that is constantly cracking jokes, punctuating that you say...or let's take them one by one, the classroom clown. You say something; he punctuates it with a silly, irrelevant joke, or he'll ask you a question that throws off the whole focus of what you are talking about, and does it purposely. It doesn't have anything to do with anything. How do you handle the classroom clown?

**M.B.** Depending on the classroom size and the situation, definitely, I say that classroom clowns, you need to get them away from their audience. Once they are away from their audience...

**Q:** And how do you do that?

**M.B.** Usually, I'll step into the hallway with them, and I have a private conference. As soon as we have a private conference, and get things cleared, they usually return back to class, and they are fine. If not, then I will talk to their parents. But it usually doesn't go to that extent.

**Q:** Okay, well as we know, a lot of times most substitute who go in for one day and don't have the parent's number, but you're saying that outside-of-the-hall conference, as you pull them aside, usually would be enough?

**M.B.** Usually. Usually. If me addressing it quickly in class does not work, then I pull them outside. If that doesn't work, and that usually does work, then they are removed and sent to the dean's office.

**Q:** Now here's another situation. You have a class, and mostly it's in middle school sometimes like the early years of high school, like ninth grade when they haven't actually made the mental psychological transition from middle school. They still have that trail of the middle school mentality into high school, and you have noisy class. You walk in, in a school you have been to before; you are there for the first time. You walk in, and nobody is paying attention to you. Everybody's talking. They're walking around. They're giggling. You're trying to give instructions. It's almost as though you're not there. Nobody is paying a word of attention to you. What do you do?

**M.B.** Well, it usually pays to have a loud voice. Luckily, I can project. I have kind of a booming voice. I will usually call attention to the

*"Some things have to be believed to be seen."–Ralph Hodgson*

class. I will raise my voice.

**Q:** Tell me exactly what you would say, please.

**M.B.**     At first, I will watch the class, and if they do not see me, and they do not get into attention, then I would raise my voice and I would say, "Class." I would say, "Class" first. And if I would say, "Class" again, and they still don't...I usually go up to three, then I would raise my voice, but usually after the second "Class", they get attention, and then I sit them down, and then we get started.

**Q:** Now you say you sit them down. Did you make them stand up at that point?

**M.B.**     Well, no, they sit down. If they're like...if it's chaos, if they're running around, and depending on the age group and the classroom situation, if they're sitting down and being noisy, then I make them stand up, and those who are quiet, then they can sit down.

**Q:** Let's go over that again. So if they're standing up, you make them sit down. If they're sitting down, you make them stand up? How long would you make them stand up?

**M.B.**     Not too long. Probably until they're quiet, then I make them sit down. Because usually what I've found out is when a student is doing something disruptive, just the change of their physical body is what it takes for them to sort of clear up and come to attention.

**Q:** Now you have a kid who is desk tapping or paper throwing. What do you do with that kid?

**M.B.**     Desk tapping and paper throwing? Well, I address that really quick.

**Q:** Okay, let's say he's tapping on the desk. *Thump. Thump-Thump. Thump. Thump-Thump-Thump.* That gets on my nerves, and I handle it swiftly. What do you do?

**M.B.**     Well, I would call on that student, and I would ask him to stop, if they continue, I will let know *why* they should not tap...

**Q:** Now you're addressing this person in front of the class?

**M.B.**     Yes, I'm addressing him in front of the class.

**Q:** And what are you saying again?

**M.B.**     I will address that they should not be tapping, why they should

*"Look well into thyself; there is a source which will always spring up if thou wilt search there."–Marcus Aurelius*

123

not be tapping, it's a disruption; I am not able to *teach* while they are tapping; they're not able to learn while they're tapping, and that's not why their parents have sent them to the classroom.

**Q:** And if they continue?

**M.B.** If they *continue* to tap, then they will get either detention after school and lunch time, or campus beautification. So, I usually give a warning, and that if they continue, they will have lunch detention, or conference with me after school, and I will call their parents. It usually doesn't get to that extent. They see that...the warnings are usually enough.

**Q:** Now this is something that *every* sub goes through, and go through this every time I go to a new school. "Uh, Mr. Bowerbank, I need to go to the restroom please?"

**M.B.** *(Laughter.)* My rule is no bathroom passes unless it's an emergency. And I've been doing it long enough, and I'm surely you probably have been too, that you can tell when it is an emergency. So, I tell them as soon as I come in that I don't give passes for any reason, that their passing period is there for them to use the restroom and get a drink, and if they did not use the restroom and get a drink, they will not be using it until the next *passing* period.

**Q:** My technique is basically, I always tell them no when they ask me for the restroom pass, and the thing is, I let them go back to their seat, and if just shrug their shoulders and continue as though nothing happened, it probably was a lie. If they come *back* to me with a nervous look on their face, trembling and shivering, and insisting, it's probably the truth, and then I'll let them go. But on the first call, I will *never* let them go. So we're pretty much on the same page with that. Now, shifting gears a bit. That conference period, when you have that extra hour, when it's free for you to do as you wish, or on the shortened days where you have shorter days, such as on minimum days, how do you like to handle your conference period and you minimum days and your shortened days when you have all that time for yourself?

**M.B.** Well, it depends on the school. Some schools, you don't have a conference period. Some schools they fill it with you going to another classroom and filling that classroom. Some schools, if you have a shortened day, you have to check into the office, and they will give you work to do. If it's a school that leaves that free time to you, I usually look through the lesson plan for the next period. I'll re-evaluate what worked and what didn't work. Sometimes I will write a report for the teacher of the previous period. Sometimes I'll tweak a lesson to sort of better institute comprehension and learning, that I think would work. That's what I would do if I had it free.

*"Anything worth doing is worth doing lousy. Just do something. Anything. Make corrections later."–Anonymous*

**Q:** Now home room is a phenomena, that I understand the theory behind it, that's it's supposed to be on the part of the students, thought gathering time where they're supposed to get their day together. What is your perspective of homeroom? How do you handle it, and what's the rule that you maintain when you are in the homeroom?

**M.B.**    I usually enforce reading in homeroom. If there are announcements because sometimes you'll get slips of paper from the office or there's a daily report, or student report for student council, something that you have to let the students know what's going on throughout the day, I'll read that. I'll read the announcements. And if there's actually time, that'll be time for reading. And, I do enforce that.

**Q:** So, you don't allow noisy homerooms?

**M.B.**    No.

**Q:** Now, teaching long term, long term subbing. What are the pros and cons of long term subbing?

**M.B.**    First I'll go with the pros. The pros of long term subbing, initially of course it makes you think of the pay increase. You get paid pretty well for accepting a long term assignment. The other benefit is your with a group of students that you get to know. You sort of... it's kind of your own mini permanent classroom, and you get to create lesson plans unless the teacher has given you lessons for the whole long term assignment. Usually you get to sort of work out your lesson planning muscles, and it's your own sort of prototype classroom for that period of time. So, you get to be the teacher, the permanent teacher in that time, so that's a positive.

**Q:** Are their any downsides?

**M.B.**    The con side is the flexibility. *(Laughter)* As a sub, you are to free not to work when you don't won't to work, or you have that diversity of going to a different classroom, or going to a different school, and with a permanent long term position, you don't have that freedom.

**Q:** Also you get out of circulation for people that request you.

**M.B.**    Exactly.

**Q:** And that kind of puts a damper when you come back in circulation, they're use to not calling you.

**M.B.**    Exactly. I've lost some connections with other schools because

*"Hold fast to dreams for if dreams die, life is a broken-winged bird that cannot fly."–Langston Hughes*

I've been at the same school for so long.

**Q:** **What is your feeling, do you like long term, or do you like day to day?**

**M.B.**    Umm. That's a good question.  I think depending on the classroom.  If it's a classroom that I really have bonds with, you know, the kids are really receptive; they want to learn; they're eager to learn; they're motivated, I'm going to enjoy the assignment more, and if it is with a subject area that I am knowledgeable about, I going to want it more, versus a classroom demographic that I don't feel equipped to handle, the subject area is not my specialty...

**Q:** **Or if it's really a difficult class that you have to deal with on a daily basis.**

**M.B.**    Exactly.

**Q:** **So, you would tend to not to like to go on and on with that particular class?**

**M.B.**    Yes, but, I am a person that likes challenges, so I would definitely go for it.  Go for the adventure, go for the challenge, and *make* it work.

**Q:** **What is your advice on handling special ed classes?  What can you give the novice entering into the world of substitute teaching about special ed classes?  What is your perspective and your insight or *tip* on handling a special ed class that you find yourself into.**

**M.B.**    Well, interestingly, I started off in a special ed classroom and with mostly special ed kids; that's a good question.  I would say that my first thing is don't take it personally.

**Q:** **What do you mean?**

**M.B.**    *(Laughter)*  I mean that kids will say and do the darndest things.  They can do some things that are just outrageous and awful.  But they can also do things that are really great and amazing.  And so I think with special ed kids, you have to keep an open mind and be *very* flexible.  You have to give them structure, but that structure has to be somewhat flexible because you may have a classroom of kids that have different learning capacities.  You might have someone that has an emotional impairment.  You might have a kid that has a physical impairment.  You may a student who cannot read.  You may have a kid who might be really advanced but slow in comprehension.  And they're all going to be in the same classroom.  So, you kind of have to be a jack of

*"Every problem contains the seeds of its own solution."–*
*Stanley Arnold*

all trades.  You have to be patient.  And so if they do not take things personal, they're flexible but give structure, and if they're patient, I think they can excel.

**Q:** So you would say that you enjoy doing special ed classes?

**M.B.**   Yes, I do.  I do.

**Q:** Now, substitute teaching, if a person wants to do this all the time, is not going to be very successful if they don't work pretty much everyday.  I have noticed that you work everyday, and I'd like you to give us some tips for the novice on how should a person go about promoting themselves so that they find themselves working everyday or as many days as possible in the schools where they would like to work in.  What's your secret for being at the same school practically everyday, and how could someone else get into the position where they're being called at a particular school that they like, and want to continue to be there.  What would you say to a person who wants to focus on a particular school and not be called all over the place?

**M.B.**   Well, getting into a particular site, I think that have to be open to whatever classroom that the office manager places them in, and so you cannot be picky.  You cannot complain.  You cannot be hard to deal with.  *(Laughter.)*

*"God doesn't make orange juice.  God makes oranges."–*
*Jesse Jackson*

**Q:** And you can't say, "I don't want to cover this class?"

**M.B.**   Exactly.  Beggars can't be choosers.  If you want to lead a horse to water, you're not going to use vinegar.  You have to use something sweet.  That substitute must be a pleasant person.  They must be open.  They must be sweet.  And your office manager is your best friend. *(Laughter.)*  So, if she puts you in a special ed class, you know, with the kids jumping off the walls, throwing erasers and everybody knows it, you'd better be the first one to say, "You know what, I'll take that class."

**Q:** Now, that's an interesting segway, because I was about to ask you, some subs call that the nightmare class when it's totally out of control.  It's that particular type of special ed where the students are not only unable to learn as quickly, but they have emotional problems as well.  And sometimes the class is a little bit larger than sort of the more autistic type of special ed where you have four or five TA's to handle three or four students.  In that huge class where the students are really, really dysfunctional and physically unable to control themselves, and they're running around and going crazy, and even raising your voice doesn't appear to help, what do you suggest to a substitute teacher that walks into class that's just surreal with disorder and chaos, and maybe there's not even a TA on that day.

**What do you do?**

**M.B.**    Usually what works is that I use reverse psychology, and that's where... it's kind of like what police do when they are disarming someone who is aggressive, like and they are caring a lethal weapon.  If someone is screaming, then you're going to do the direct opposite.  You're going to talk calmly, because that calm voice is going to de-escalate the situation.

**Q:** So you don't need screaming with screaming?

**M.B.**    Exactly.  You have to use your voice in the right particular time.  If you have a student that's just belligerent, that is loud, that is demanding, *you* want to do the direct opposite.  You want to be calm.  You want to be laid back.  You want to not be aggressive because they are just going to rise and be aggressive to you.  So usually what I have found out especially in special education situations is that if you can de-escalate the situation, you're going to be a success.

**Q:** Now, I had seen you once in action where it was a library situation where you were watching the kids, and there was this one girl who confronted you, and spoke to you with some disrespect, I saw you almost bite her head off...verbally.  Is that a contradiction to what you just said to me in terms of de-escalating and becoming calmer?

**M.B.**    No, because I knew that girl.  I've seen her.  I kind of know her.  I kind of know how she works and how she deals, and how she intimidates people.  And on the reverse side, it's kind of like a double-edged sword, sometimes if you have a dog, let's say a chihuahua with loud bark, sometimes you need a rockwelder *(laughter)* to put that chihuahua in its place.

*"We are the wire, God is the current.  Our only power is to let the current pass through us."–Carlo Carretto*

**Q:** So you were a rockwelder on that day?  *(Laughter).*

**M.B.**    Yeah, I felt like she was definitely grandstanding, and she was a chihuahua with a loud bark.  So I just had to show her that there's a little bit of a bigger dog that deserves more respect.  And that's one thing I do not tolerate.  I do not tolerate when students disrespect.  The method of how I address it may change, but with her she was definitely someone who needed to see the rockwelder.  *(Laughter.)*

**Q:** Interesting, I like your metaphor.  Final question, the gifted class, the honors class, what is your perspective, your experience and your approach in handling this class?

**M.B.**    Hmmm.  Well, it's interesting, sometimes the gifted students or students that may perceive themselves as gifted or they're placed in a gifted class, sometimes I have situations where you'll have problems *of* disrespect. You'll have problems where they...

**Q:** They think they're clever enough to get away with it.

**M.B.**    Exactly. And so I don't change in my method of...

**Q:** So you don't drop your guard down, so to speak, just because they called themselves gifted?

**M.B.**    Exactly. The method of teaching may change. The method of the way I bring across information...I may move quicker with them, but school rules, school policy, classroom rules, classroom policies are... they still need to adhere to.

**Q:** Interesting. Now, in summary, Mr. Bowerbank, there is a new substitute teacher right now who is reading your words and looking up to you as one who is the experience person leading the way, blazing the trail of substitute teaching as a profession, what would be your advice in general to that person who aspires to make substitute teaching a career?

*"Belief is the only door through which the power of God can flow."–Charles Prosper*

**M.B.**    Hmmm. I would tell them the golden rule of enjoy it. Enjoy it. Be sure that you're doing something you enjoy doing. Don't take everything seriously. Be flexible. Be personal. Go the extra mile. Be patient. And work with the teachers, and work with the students, and talk to the office manager. Be pleasant. Anything positive that you can do to make the experience better, I would definitely say do it. And if you're positive, I always tell the kids, a happy teacher is a happy classroom. And it's works in vice versa, happy students make a happy experience for the teacher. So if you walk into a classroom and you're positive, and you go in there and say I'm going to have a great day, I'm here to make a difference, you're going to have a better experience. That's is what I would tell them.

**Q:** Excellent. Well, we appreciate your experience, your wisdom and your words, and I'm sure a lot of people are going to be inspired by your advice. And I thank you so much for this interview.

**M.B.**    Well thank you for interviewing me.

Wow! I don't know about you, but that was a pretty inspiring interview even for me in spite of all of my experience. Mark Bowerbank is without doubt, one of the best in the profession of substitute teaching *par excellence.* But hold on to your seats because coming up next is a powerhouse of substitute knowledge and ability, Louie Alcaraz.

## Louie Alcaráz (Super Sub)

**Q:** We are with Mr. Louie Alcaráz today. Mr. Alcaráz don't they call you something else here?

**L.A.**   Yes, they do. Students call me Mr. A. A lot of people tell me it's kind of tacky, *(laughter)* but you know I tell them when it's short and crisp, they remember you.

**Q:** Well, I appreciate you participating and being a part of this, hopefully, classic work on substitute teaching. It's never been done before like this, and so I am just creaming the best subs that I know of, and I consider you one of them. And I admire you and, I've watched you, and I know when anybody is here everyday is here for a reason. And so, Mr. A, why are you a sub? Why become a sub, and what is your general substitute philosophy?

**L.A.**   First of all, I love teaching. I've been doing this for about three years. Actually, the majority of my family members, for example, my mother, my brother, my younger sister, aunts, uncles are teachers. I had been in a classroom way before I started working at this middle school, and I just love to teach and come from the heart.

*"To believe with certainty, we must begin without doubting."–Charles Prosper*

**Q:** Well, the question I always get is why you're not a full-time teacher, Mr. Prosper? I always get that. So, why is it that you're subbing? Why you're not a full-time teacher?

**L.A.**   Okay, right now, the reason I am not teaching (full-time) right now is because I also play baseball.

**Q:** So, it allows you to do other things.

**L.A.**   Exactly, it gives me that freedom to do other things, and, you know, I like the freedom.

**Q:** And I think that's a reason why a lot of us become subs like myself. I like the freedom to have other things in addition to teaching. The question I always get as well is "Yeah, but it's not as secure as 'real' teachers" quote, unquote. I mean, is substitute teaching secure?

**L.A.**   Well, depends. It depends. I think in my opinion, it is, but you have to establish yourself. For example...

**Q:** And how do you do that?

**L.A.**   How do I do that, well I remember when I first started working here at this middle school, I was a tutor for another teacher, about, about say two years, and I got to know a lot of teachers. So, I was working for not only this particular teacher but many other teachers as well, and that's how I began liking it, because I didn't have my degree yet, my bachelors degree, and just my family members, the majority of them being teachers...I was born to teach...

**Q:** But specifically the person who is reading your words right now is asking, "Well, how do I get myself known? I mean, you're well known. They call you everyday, but I'm just starting. I don't know anything about getting into the loop of them calling me. What's the first thing I would do? I'm a new person who wants to be as good as you are. How do I get known? How do I get them calling me everyday?

**L.A.** First of all, right after I became a sub, I knew the office manager real well. So, that always helps. Sometimes, but not all the time, it's who you know. Like I say, you have to establish yourself. For example, I still remember the first day I taught. I was in a classroom. I remember I had an aide, and word spreads. Word spreads. It took a while, because at the beginning, I would say they would call me in about, an average about 3 times a week. Three times a week. So, it took about, I would say, six months, a good six, seven months, you know after word starting spreading...

*"What you can do, or dream you can do, begin it; boldness has genius, power and magic in it."–Johann von Goethe*

**Q:** And then you go pretty much everyday?

**L.A.** Exactly.

**Q:** And is this the only school where you work in?

**L.A.** Right now, yes.

**Q:** And you pretty much work everyday?

**L.A.** I say about 90 to 95% of the time?

**Q:** And that's what people don't understand when I tell them, it is as secure as you want it to be. I mean, it's a full-time job if you want it to be. And we get the same benefits if you work enough hours. And this is the myth that I want to dispel of it not being secure. You are evidence of the fact, and I know of other substitutes that are everyday, and they have just tapped into the secret. It's a quiet little secret that once you're well known and established, and you *want* to work everyday, and you want to be at a certain school, you probably find yourself in that school. Hasn't that been your experience?

**L.A.** I think so. Exactly.

**Q:** Now, I want to shift gears a bit, and go into the actual heart of the classroom. We know that there's a lot of benefits of being a substitute teacher, the freedom to able to do other things other than subbing once you call it a day, but when you're in the classroom, if it were that easy, everybody would be doing it, and one of the key things that keeps people from being a sub is the fact of the discipline problems. I mean, it's rough! It's rough. They don't know. You don't know them. You're scoping them out. They're scoping you out. It's like cat and mouse. They figure, "I want to get over on this sub. This is *our* class, and *he's* the intruder." And you're scoping them out, "You're not going to take over this class because *I'm* the teacher. So, your both playing this psychological cat and mouse game in the first two or three minutes. My first question is this, does "nice" work?

**L.A.**    I don't think so. It works at times, but, let's say for example, I've been here at this school working on a regular basis, they know I'm nice, but they also know I can be real mean. So, that's going to depend on them. First of all, I think it's real important, if it's a new school that you're going to, it's real important to dress nice, your dress tie. Second of all, I never, I never smile. Okay. I never smile, and I think that's *key*.

*"Our remedies oft in ourselves do lie."–William Shakespeare*

**Q:** Excuse me for interrupting you, but that's one of the first things that *I* say when people ask me. I walk in, and I say the same thing, I don't even smile. Isn't that interesting that we have that same mind-set? And why is that? *I* know the answer why, but you tell me why?

**L.A.**    I don't smile because...the reason I don't smile...I get a feeling that when they see me, the kids know right away that I mean business. That's my reason.

**Q:** I agree with you. I agree with you. In fact it is so interesting that you even said before I was going to ask you the question. I had it as one of my questions, do you smile or not smile. That's shows that certain principles work, and we discover them independently even before we talk about them. So, yeah, I agree with you on that. We're on the same page with that. Now, here's another question, to shout or not to shout, that is the question?

**L.A.**    It's necessary at times. I hate to do it. I know it takes a lot of my energy, but I when I do it, I get the kids attention. So at times it is necessary.

**Q:** And in what cases would you do it?

**L.A.**    Ah, when the kid repeatedly, misbehaves, not doing their work, and I constantly have to remind them to not be disruptive, for example, and if it doesn't work, I have to kick them out of class. Call up a teacher or call up a dean.

**Q:** And for example, how do you handle defiance? A student says, like, I had the other day, I had a pretty rough class. Well, special day classes are usually difficult, but let's say in a regular class you get a student who is defiant and tells you they don't care what you say, or they're *not* going to do. They just outright say, " I don't care. I'm not going to do it."

**L.A.**    I think the kid is testing me, especially being a sub. So what I do, how I handle it is I don't say anything. What I do, I have the student, I kick him out of class, and I go talk to him, with the door open, I go to him...for a few minutes...

**Q:** Do you want anybody else to hear you?

**L.A.**    I don't want anyone else to hear me...because...actually I don't want to raise my voice at that time. But I think I'm better off kicking the student out, having a word with him. If it *helps,* then good! If it doesn't help...you know, I don't tolerate that. I don't tolerate it. I'll just call up the dean. I hate writing referrals. I know we have to. It's necessary. I've been here for a while, and well, I'll try to work with the student. I'll try to work with the student and I'll tell him, "You know what, I tell you what..." I don't really believe in rewards, but it's necessary at times, and I'll talk to him and I'll pull him aside, and "I'll talk him outside, take him outside, "You know what, if you do this..." Let's say, for example, this is a math class, I'll ask them, "If you don't want to do it, what do *you* want to do? What do you guys want to do?" And, I'll let them respond. I'll give them that freedom.

**Q:** What if they say they don't want to do anything?

**L.A.**    If they say, "I don't want to do nothing," okay, I'll let them. They will do *nothing.*

**Q:** Really?

**L.A.**    Listen. If I know if I'm going to be in this class for, say, three days, and the kid says, and is being defiant or tells me, "I don't want to do nothing," so what I'll do instead, I will ask every student. I'll ask them, "What do you want to do today? *Nothing.*" I'll ask the next student, "What do you want to do? *I'll do some work.*" Okay, that's one "work". And I move on. And let's say I get about...70% of the class who don't want to do anything...so what I'll do...they will do absolutely *nothing!* For fifty minutes...for the whole class...

**Q:** What do you mean absolutely nothing?

*"We will either find a way, or make one."–Hannibal*

**L.A.**    What I is mean is that...I know I'm going to come back tomorrow, so that means I going to give them zero's.  And I'll let their teacher know, that they did *nothing* for the whole period.  The next day, I'll ask them the same question.  That's the first thing when I walk in, I'll ask them the same question...you know what's that's going to do?

**Q:** Now, when you say, let them do nothing... I can't picture this because they are going to be chatty...

**L.A.**    They're going to do *nothing*...

**Q:** I can't picture this because they are going to be chatty...

**L.A.**    That's what I'm saying, *"Uh, Mister?"* I say, "No, no, no, hold on.  You're talking.  You told me..." *"Uh, Mister, could."* They pull out a book.  They pull out a book and start reading.  "What are you doing?"  For example, I had this happen in an English class where at the beginning I had the students where they were reading silently.  And I say about thirty percent of them were reading.  After that I asked them the question, and seventy percent of the class was doing nothing, and that's going to bore you.

**Q:** When you say nothing, you literally mean...

**L.A.**    *Nothing!*

**Q:** They can't talk...

**L.A.**    They can't *talk!* They can't *read!* They can't do *anything!* They can't *write...*

**Q:** They can't scratch their heads...

**L.A.**    They can't *anything!* Period.

**Q:** They have to sit there with their hands on their laps?

**L.A.**    Exactly!  And they get tired.  So, eventually, they're going to tell me, *"Uh, Mister..."* and they pull out their book.  "Oh, now you want to read?  Oh no, no, no!  You told me you wanted to do nothing."

**Q:** Hmm.

**L.A.**    Okay, so the next day, when they know I'm coming back, I ask the same question.  I ask the same question to every student.  And they're

*"I finally figured out the only reason to be alive is to enjoy it."–Rita Mae Brown*

going to get tired. They're going to say, *"Oh, Mister, I'm bored..."* and this and that. "Oh no, you can't do it because that what you told me. You want to do nothing? You're not going to do anything today. So the next day, I ask every student, and I get one hundred percent of the students to read their book. Every student told me that they wanted to do some work. "But what do you want to do today?" *"I want to do some work. I want to read my book."*

**Q:** Hmm. Unique. I had never heard of that. That's absolutely brilliant. That had never occurred to me, but after all that's why I'm picking the brains of the best in the business, the best in the business of subbing. Now on that same line, this is so unique. I find it so fascinating because it had never occurred to me. Now the students that say they want to do some work, do you allow them to do work?

**L.A.** Oh, I allow them...if they want to do some work.

**Q:** But the ones who say they want to do nothing, do you separate them in a little group by themselves?

**L.A.** I leave them there right next to the students who are reading books.

**Q:** But they have to sit down and look at the wall?

**L.A.** They sit down and look at the wall and do *nothing!*

**Q:** And if they attempt to do anything?

**L.A.** I'll let them know. I'm observing.

**Q:** And if they become fidgety, and they insist – there's *even* consequences for doing *nothing!*

**L.A.** Of course. There's already consequences to begin with. They get a zero – an "F" for the day. I think that's enough.

**Q:** So, in other words, if you insist on *not* doing *nothing,* you're going to get me on your case because that what we agreed to. That was our agreement.

**L.A.** That was our agreement. Exactly.

**Q:** And you've found this to work?

**L.A.** It's worked so far.

*"Results are what you expect; consequences are what you get."–Anonymous*

135

**Q:** Beautiful. Beautiful. Absolutely beautiful. Now, there is a couple of standard situations that I want to ask you about before I come into some of the other ones. This is one that almost every new sub will get when he walks into a class. I've had four or five students ask me this in the first ten minutes when they don't know who I am and what I stand for. "Uh, Mister, Mr. Prosper, can I go to the restroom? Mr. A, can I go to the restroom?" What your response to that?

**L.A.**     Well, it depends. Depends. You know, I let them know right off the bat. I tell them, "You know what..." because I get this all the time especially at the beginning of the class or towards the end of class. So what I do, I let them know right away, the school policy. I go, "You know what, during the first or the last ten minutes of class, I can't let you guys go to the restroom. Period."

**Q:** You let that be known in the beginning?

**L.A.**     And, if there here, let's say for example, it's my third period, and my fifth period class, it is rare that I let them go to the restroom. Why? Because they just had nutrition, and they just had lunch. Okay? But sometimes, it's an emergency. So I test them. I test them.

**Q:** How do you know if it's an emergency?

**L.A.**     I test them. I go, "You know what, I'll let you go in about ten minutes." If they're serious, they're going to remember. And if they're not, you can tell. You can tell if it's an emergency or not.

**Q:** How can you tell?

**L.A.**     Or else, I 'll tell them, "You know what, I'll let you go..." let's say they are working at the beginning of the class because I always have them do a warm-up. You know, I'll let some go, but I'll tell them, "I tell you what, do these first four or five problems, and I'll let you go." I don't have a problem with that. If they do the problems, then I know it's serious. But, I test them at times. I test them because it's always those same students. It's always the same students...

**Q:** I have even had them to tell me, "Well, I always go out to the restroom!" *(Laughter)*

**L.A.**     Or sometimes I'll tell them, I'll tell them. I go, "You know what *I* have to go to the restroom—but I *can't!* That's why I always make sure when I go to nutrition or during my passing period, I go to the restroom." But you know, you can see when the kids are shaking, when they tell you about five or six times, "Mister, I really, really need to go,"

*"We pray to God that He may answer our prayer, and God prays to us that we may believe–so that we may receive that which we pray for."–Charles Prosper*

you let them go.

**Q:** Now before I shift gears to some other questions, I have had many classes when I walk in, and everybody is talking. I'm standing up, and I'm trying to get their attention, and it's like you're not even there. You're invisible. I'm trying to explain, and it's like five or six conversations going on at once. What do you say? What is your vocal alarm that you use to get their attention?

**L.A.**    First of all, I don't say anything. I don't say anything. Okay? Sometimes, I just give them a serious look. It works, at times. I will say it hasn't worked all the time. Sometimes when you give them that serious look. And I'll cross my arms...

**Q:** You'll stand up and won't say anything?

**L.A.**    I won't say anything, and eventually the students will just stare at me, and I'll give them the serious look, and they'll start talking to each other, "Okay. Shut up. Alright. Be quiet." Because they know I'm mad. They know I'm upset. If it doesn't work, and they keep on talking, what I do—*I shut off the lights.* I shut it off until they're good and quiet. If they're not quiet, if that doesn't work, what I do, I'll treat them like kindergarten or elementary students, I shut off the lights and have them put their heads down.

**Q:** *Really?*

**L.A.**    And it works! And I let them know, "You know what, put your heads down! Put your heads down!"

**Q:** What grade level?

**L.A.**    It's worked with 6th graders. It's works real well with 6th graders. With 7th and 8th, I hate to do that, but sometimes it's necessary. With 8th and 7th, I'm more flexible, or I'll even raise my voice. But the lights, it helps. When you shut off the lights, it helps. With the 7th and 8th graders, it helps. With 6th graders, it's worked all the time.

**Q:** Fascinating.

**L.A.**    And they put their heads down, I get their attention.

**Q:** That's fascinating. I've never, never used that particular technique. Absolutely fascinating. Wow, this is really, really eye-opening even to me and all of my years doing this. Now here's a very

*"The purpose of life is a life of purpose."–Robert Byrne*

**important question I need to ask you of the ones that come up when substitute teachers talk to me about the situations. What happens when you walk into a class...how do you handle no lesson plans?**

**L.A.**    No lesson plans. That's a good one. First of all, I always carry emergency lesson plans–for every subject–and sometimes if there's an aide, I'll ask the aide.

Let's say for example, let's say I walk into a math class, there's always something to do for math–always! Or, I'll even ask some of the students, what chapter they're on, what they're doing, and I'll get some help that way, but what I'll do if there's a roll book, and if the teacher gives me permission to look in her roll book, and look at what they are working on. Like I said before, ask the students. I'll come up with some problems, and give them a lesson plan that way. But, I've never had a problem with that. But, it's starts way before you enter a classroom. I always expect the worst. I know I have to get a good night's rest because it's important. Come prepared.

It's like for example, I'm a shortstop, and I have to work with the second baseman. On double plays, when he gets a ground ball, and feed me the ball, I expect the bat-throw because if I don't expect the bat-throw, and he makes a bat-throw, that's when it's going to catch me by surprise, and that's when I'm going to commit the error, or I'm going to break down.

So I will always expect the worst, but I'm very optimistic. And, I'll even ask the students, and I'll be honest and let them know, your teacher did not leave a lesson plan, so I'll leave it up to you guys, what do you guys want to do today? But it has to be related to obviously the same project that they're working on. *(Laughter.)* I'll be flexible. So, I'll give them that freedom.

**Q:** **What do you think about movies?**

**L.A.**    Oh movies! Oh, I was going there. I don't like movies, but sometimes it's necessary. For example, like last year I had this one class, I don't want to mention any names, but it was those *same* students that *you* had! *(Laughter.)* You know who they are.

**Q:** **Yeah, I know who they are.** *(Laughter.)*

**L.A.**    So what I did...I carry a movie with me all the time, just in case all fails.

**Q:** **What kind of movie?**

**L.A.**    Well, I love National Geographic. If that doesn't work, and if I notice it kind of bores students, so what I'll do is call up the librarian because they have movies and ask them what kind of movie should I show these kids. They know most of the kids, and I'll explain, and I'll tell them about my situation, and we'll go from there. Sometimes I'll even show, let's say for example, SpongeBob if I have to, just to get their attention. So, it depends on the kids. I look at them, and if they're talking about Jordan, basketball, I'll show them a movie, let's say for example, like *Be Like Mike*. Now I know that's going to get their attention. That's if all fails. It worked with *that* class. *(Laughter.)*

**Q:** Sometimes you would use movies as a diversion, as a tranquilizer, just an attention getter, that kind of thing?

**L.A.**    I think so. If all fails.

**Q:** Now so, in essence, this would be with classes that are like extremely, extremely difficult?

**L.A.**    *Extremely* difficult.

**Q:** Okay, and you just need to get them, their attention off of just being disruptive, and you get them focused on the movie. And sometimes I find that you even have to work at it just to make them sit down and watch the movie.

*"He who fears he shall suffer already suffers what he fears."—Michel de Montaigne*

**L.A.**    Exactly. Especially if the kids are coming from, right after nutrition, and after lunch because the kids, with all this food and all this caffeine that they're consuming...which is understandable. Nothing wrong with that, so I'll give them like five minutes just to calm down. Calm down. Calm down. Calm down. And if I lose them, then I have to do what I have to do. I'll do the "shut off the lights".

**Q:** Yes. Right. Right, right, right. Okay, in wrapping things up. The last question I would like to ask you would be what's your experience with the gifted class, the high achieving classes. What is your experience with them?

**L.A.**    Oh, I love, I love to cover those classes because I think...

**Q:** Any behavior problems?

**L.A.**    Uh, at times.

**Q:** And do you handle them any differently?

**L.A.**    I do handle them differently, but I don't have a problem with them. Basically, they can run the class. Those days are just fascinating. I'm so impressed because the majority of these classes at this school, they love doing those Cornell notes. I don't know if you're familiar with them. And, these guys are good! They are very good. Excellent note takers. I never used to take notes like that. Now I do. But, it's like I say, I never have major, major problems, but when I do, I still have that energy to...what I'm trying to say is that they're manageable.

**Q.** My experience is also been the same that if there is a problem, they quickly tighten up again. You say, "Okay, look, I don't want to have to tell your teacher that you're..." *"Oh, I'm sorry, Mr. Prosper!"* And so that they'll get a little loose. You talk to them, and them they'll tighten up really easy. So you don't spend a lot of energy to tighten them up and to get them focused. And that's been my experience as well.

Well, Mr. A, this has been an exciting interview, I mean, *I* have learned something as I was expecting to. Any final words for that person aspiring to be a substitute teacher?

**L.A.** Oh, yes, yes, yes. I used to fear, because I took a classroom management class, at Cal State L.A., and I was very scared, just to...I still remember my first day. I was real scared, and it was interesting because I was already in a classroom as a math tutor...but I think it begins way before you enter a classroom, for example, get a good night's sleep. Eat your breakfast. Dress up a bit. Make sure you're feeling good, looking good and have the energy to do the class.

Always leave a note. *(Laughter.)* Always leave a note. Let the teacher know...I don't care if they don't leave a lesson plan...you leave a note anyway. When you leave, make sure...I mean, I like to have the classroom clean. I know it's not my classroom, but, it's just me. This is just me. That's the way I am. And, finally, when I do leave, be proud of yourself and what you do! And when you sign out, make sure to let the office manager know how your day went. Leave them your business card, and tell them, let them know, that if you ever need me...and word spreads, word spreads, and eventually word spreads.

**Q.** Well, Mr. A, I appreciate this interview. It's been enlightening for me. I 've learned something...*I'm* going to try some of your techniques out *tomorrow! (Laughter.)* Tomorrow!

I see why you're here everyday, and I really appreciate this, and everybody listening to your words of wisdom are going to benefit from this as well, and so you're going to help many other people all over the country to be as good as you are. I thank you.

**L.A.** I hope so. I hope so.

**Q.** Thank you very much.

**L.A.** Alright.

*"Forgiveness is the sweetest revenge."–Isaac Friedmann*

Mr. A is A-1. Our third and final super sub interview is with a sub that I have admired for the last 2 years, for a couple of reasons. One, he is unusually soft spoken, in most cases. Very relaxed and kicked back. But the amazing thing about Art Resendez is that he usually accepts long term sub positions, back to back, and usually they are the *most* difficult classes in the entire school. I'm talking about entire classes of students that are vulgar, disruptive, potentially violent and even some with fringe associations with gangs. He is like the fireman. Everybody else is running *out* of the burning building, and he is the only one who is running *in!* He is like, if there is anyone to whom this label could be attributed, the Zen master of substitute teaching. Let us now enter into the fascinating world of super sub, Art Resendiz.

## Art Resendiz (Super Sub)

**Q:** Mr. Resendez, I'm going to ask you some questions here. First of all the people that would be reading this would be asking, "Why become a substitute teacher? Why would anybody want to become a substitute teacher? What's your response to that?

**A.R.**   I think it would be for people who are interested in teaching and are not certain about it. They might want to get their feet wet in a sense. Check out want substitute teaching is about. And at that point, they can probably decide if they want to continue with substitute teaching or teaching itself or quit the profession altogether.

**Q:** In kind of like one, two, three manner, what are the advantages of subbing, and what are the disadvantages of subbing?

**A.R.**   Oh, let me see. The advantages of that are when you get to get a chance to observe, to be in the classroom, to be an active teacher in a sense if you're interested in becoming a teacher. And, disadvantage of subbing is pay *(a chuckle)*. You get paid less than a regular teacher. Another disadvantage would be the fact because you are the substitute that the students sometimes would see that as holiday for them, and they'll try to...

**Q:** Why are *you* a sub? Why are you a substitute teacher? What keeps you as a substitute teacher? What's your main goal and motivation to be a substitute teacher? Because I know you're here all the time, and so there must be a reason why you're here.

**A.R.**   Well, originally it stems from just liking kids. I've been working with kids for about fifteen years already, started out as a TA (teacher's aide), and I'm still on my way to becoming a teacher so this kind of keeps me related to what I like–working with kids.

*"We carry with us the wonders we seek without us."–Sir Thomas Browne*

141

**Q:** So you're ultimate goal is to become a full-time teacher?

**A.R.** Ultimately, yes. *(A chuckle).*

**Q:** Now, would you say...people ask me this all the time. Is substitute teaching secure?

**A.R.** I can be, yes, but you've got to do the work. You've got to keep in touch with administration, school administration. Keep in touch with the school secretary, for example. I would go up in administration and let them know that you're available.

**Q:** Like when you say administration, who do you mean specifically?

**A.R.** Like the vice principal at this school. I would pick a school, and work with that school, or work with a series of schools–two or three schools at most versus going all over the district–that would be disastrous. It just would be very difficult. You would have to pick a school or a series of schools where you get to know administration. Let them know how good you are. You got to do your part in leaving notes for the teachers and everything. The teachers will recommend you to administration.

**Q:** And how close do you work with the girls at the front office? Are they really instrumental in getting you more jobs, or is it the administration?

**A.R.** More the secretary, in this case, in this school, Elsa. I think she's head secretary at this school. More so with her, but then eventually she is the one that let's administration know who are the top people qualified for like long-term positions which is what I after right now, other long-terms.

**Q:** And so you need, the administration is the one who gives the approval for the long-terms?

**A.R.** Most of the time, yes.

**Q:** Middle school versus high school. What is your take on that? What's the difference, or is there any difference?

**A.R.** Ah, you need more discipline and more structure in middle school than you do in high school I think. But personally, when I've gone to high school, I, personally, I've just been more bored because the students, they are usually either at a state where they're going to achieve, and they do work and when you are a substitute, they're doing their work and they don't need any help. Or, they'll be the other way where

*"Don't ask of your friends what you yourself can do."–Quintus Ennius*

they don't care about the work, and there's nothing really anything you can do to scare them or get them motivated to do the work. So, I think as long as they're quiet, I think that's...

**Q:** You find that there are no discipline problems in high school?

**A.R.** There are, but not as much I think as in middle school. I think is because of the fact that in middle school, they are still going through puberty, and this age region of twelve to fifteen, I think there's more hormonal things going inside their body than kids that are in high school.

**Q:** Now the series of questions are have to do with the key thing in being a sub, the discipline principle. The first question I always ask, does "nice" work?

**A.R.** No. It does not always work.

**Q:** And what is your approach to discipline, since you say that nice is not necessarily the way that you go? What would you advise somebody who is walking into a class as a new substitute teacher for the very first time? What is your advice to them?

**A.R.** Be firm. State *exactly* what you expect out of the students. It helps when there's a lesson plan. Let them know what's expected before they leave. What's expected in the class. You could be nice, but as long as you're firm, I think. You can be nice about it, but bottom line just be clear and be firm, and show what you expect.

**Q:** How do you handle situations, like uh, this Carlos guy that we talked about who's really, really rebellious. He makes noise. He throw backpacks. He's profane. He's disrespectful. I guess he can be confronting. And you have this guy everyday now in this long-term. How do you handle a character like this?

**A.R.** I worked with him already three days. So far I feel like I've not gotten any progress with him. Before he enters the class, we'll talk outside. I have to counsel him. I've tried the firm approach with him. Didn't work. I tried the disciplinarian approach with him, it didn't work. Then I tried the more I'm-going-to-settle-back-and-won't-be-as-strict, let me try a nicer approach, which didn't help, has not worked.

So today I'm going to try...I don't know what I'm going to try today, but I got to keep on trying to talk to him outside, and what I want him to do hopefully, maybe is try to get used to each other, and then I'm going to let him in the room—even if he is in five minutes before I throw him out. *(Chuckle.)* Some type of progress has to be occurring...

*"Faith doesn't wait until it understands; in that case it wouldn't be faith."–Vance Havner*

**Q:** Is there any point that you feel that you just can't teach, a certain person like him? Or is there a point where you just feel that he's not teachable?

**A.R.**     Uh, not yet. I think he is teachable. It's going to take a long time though. Right now, I think it's just a matter that we need to get to know each other. So, I'll let him sit in today. Hopefully, he'll go five minutes or more.

**Q:** Have you thrown him out before?

**A.R.**     Yes. I've let him inside the classroom, and he's lasted about a minute because...

**Q:** A minute?

**A.R.**     Yeah, too much profanity. Too much...and he's throws backpacks around. He climbs on the table and stuff like that...

**Q:** So, he obviously doesn't want to be here?

**A.R.**     Yes, he's got an agenda.

*"A consciousness of God releases the greatest power of all."—Science of Mind*

**Q:** He's got an agenda. Would you think that the best thing to do would be to make it easy for him not to be here, like just getting him out as quick as he starts to act up?

**A.R.**     At points like this, yes. Yes, because the other students are very influential. There's a couple of other students who are trying to do the same thing. So, I feel that if I let him get away with it, the other two will start acting up also. Soon after that I would probably have a mutiny here.

**Q:** But you seem pretty centered and pretty calm. I admire your ability to handle that situation. Most people run from classes like this. You know like the fireman that runs *into* the building while everybody else is running *out* of it.

**A.R.**     *(Laughter.)*

**Q:** "Can I go to the restroom, teacher?" First five minutes of class. What is your response to that?

**A.R.**     I've got something setup already where if they *have* to go during the class, they've got to make up the time after. So, if they take five minutes to go to the restroom, actually that's the time I give them, five minutes, after class, they've got to make up that time. And they got that option. So, if they really, really, really have to go, they'll go.

**Q:** Initially even when they ask you "Can I go?" do you usually tell them okay you can go provided that you come back in five minutes. Do you just always yes, or do you always say, "No, you can't go."

**A.R.** Sometimes I say no to them. And sometimes, depending on the type of class if it is a very loud and noisy class, where I know they want to get out, they don't won't to be there, then I strictly say no. Just because that's the feel of the class.

**Q:** So, you go by the feel of the class?

**A.R.** Um-Hm.

**Q:** Now, the classroom clown. The guy that's heckling you, you know with silly jokes and interrupting you, and just attracting the attention, trying to get everyone to laugh at him. How do you handle the class clown?

**A.R.** I'll ask him to step outside, and as soon as I'm done giving instructions for the rest of the class, I'll have *my* talk with him and tell him what I want and *don't* want from him. Like Carlos trying to get me upset, I'll tell him to stop right at that moment, or else he has to go...let him go to the dean's office.

**Q:** And you'll write him up and send him out?

**A.R.** Yes.

**Q:** Do you ever raise your voice?

**A.R.** Yes. Yes.

**Q:** Under what circumstances?

**A.R.** Under this particular case, with special ed students, they're not very quiet. You know, you give them independent work sometime, so they get very noisy. There's a certain point where you have to tell them to stop. Either they'll have to clean up or there is an announcement, announcing the next lesson, then you have to raise your voice. I'll do a counting, first like a three, two, one, and if that doesn't work, then I'll start counting names out–loudly–over there voices, and then they stop. Usually they stop.

*"You'll see it when you believe it."–Wayne Dyer*

145

**Q:** Have you ever felt yourself getting angry, or are you pretty much always in control of yourself?

**A.R.**     Uh, I do find myself getting angry sometimes, and that's the part I think I got to work on myself. I think that ideally, the ideal teacher would be the one that won't let the emotions run.

You'd have to set your system down where okay if this happens, then do this. Where you don't have to get angry, where you don't have to let your emotions get the best of you. And that's another thing I try not to do in front of the students, let them see my emotions that way. I'll laugh occasionally, but if it's a new class or a very tough class, then no. Emotions aren't part of the lesson, aren't part of the teaching, aren't part of me. So we get to know each other more I guess.

**Q:** But, you are capable of using what I call a "voice alarm" and raising your voice to get them under control.

**A.R.**     Yes.

**Q:** So, you seem to be pretty centered. You try to keep yourself under control. You raise your voice if you *have* to. And when there's a problem, you pull that person outside and have a talk. Is that pretty much your approach? Would that be correct in saying that?

**A.R.**     Yes, that's correct.

**Q:** And that has pretty much has worked for your pretty well?

**A.R.**     It's worked pretty well.

**Q:** Now, this is a question that I get oftentimes from beginning substitute teachers. What if there is no lesson plans? What do you do? This is a new sub, and he's walking into a class, and there's no lesson plans, what does he do? What is your advice to him?

**A.R.**     Ah, first of all, I carry word searches sometimes. Not whole classroom sets; maybe I'll carry one or two, or assignments based on the subject you're teaching, basic worksheet assignments, and...

**Q:** That you prepare ahead of time?

**A.R.**     That I have ahead of time.

**Q:** So basically, you don't walk into a classroom without having something in your hands?

*"If you would have a faith-ful servant, and one that you like, serve yourself."—Benja-min Franklin*

**A.R.**    Exactly.  If it's math, just carry in some kind of math sheet, even if it's just multiplication, or sometime basic, even if it's an algebra class.  I mean, but you have to have I think some kind of worksheet ready, just in case you run into situations like that, and we do as substitutes, so just be prepared.  Get that copy down to the main office.  Have copies done.  But I think you also, as a substitute teacher, have to be ready with some kind of lesson, while you're waiting for your worksheet to be copied.  Ask some basic questions.  Write them on the board.  Like a quick journal.  An assignment.  Whatever it be.  What did you do last night?  What did you do over the weekend?  Or what are your plans for...

**Q:** So basically your advice is to the new sub is don't walk in their unprepared.  Assume that the worst could happen, and always have something in your briefcase ready to fly out with a lesson.

**A.R.**    Yes.

**Q:** Okay, that sounds like good advice.  Okay, well we're wrapping down to the last couple of questions.  What is your philosophy and approach to the special ed class that's *really,* really difficult?  Pretty much like the one you are handling right now.  What would you advise someone who has never had a special ed class that's really out of control, lot of behavior problems, lot of rebelliousness, profanity and the whole thing?  What is your advice to the sub that has to take over this kind of a class?

*"Oh Lord, thou givest us everything at the price of effort."–Leonardo da Vinci*

**A.R.**    Overall–firmness.  Walk in with a lot of firmness.  Walk in with a structure with a structure.  You have to set them up with a structure.  That is make a seating chart.  Set the rules.  No profanity.  No gum.  Give them rules, and overall patience.  A lot of patience.

**Q:** Well, Mr. Resendez, we thank you a lot for this interview.  And I know a lot of people are going to be helped by your experience and insights.  And thank you so much for your time.

**A.R.**    You're welcome.

There you have it.  You have just had the rare opportunity to enter into some of the finest minds in the profession of substitute teaching.  The history of substitute teaching has not been finally written yet.  Step up to the plate.  You are the next legendary super sub.

*"Shoot for the moon, even if you miss, you will land among the stars."* –Les Brown

**CHAPTER**

# How to Handle the Special Ed Class

There is a type of substitute teaching situation that requires more care knowledge and professionalism. Many substitute teachers are no more than part-time students, "wannabee" actors, writers, singers or otherwise individuals waiting for their "ship to come in", so to speak, in another field of endeavor. Whatever other occupation a substitute teacher has his or her sights on, a total professional perspective must be taken into the situation of the Special Ed Class.

## What is a Special Ed Class

A Special Ed class addresses the needs of those students who are academically challenge alongside a wide spectrum of struggle. On the mild level, there are those students who have fallen several grade levels below the norm of the state's learning standards. On the severe level, there are the MT (mentally retarded) students who may need the cooperation and participation of other professionals as well as counselors, nurses and psychiatrists.

## The RSP Class

The first category of Special Ed is the RSP class. This stands for Resource Special Ed. An RSP class is that class where the students have fallen 1 or 2 grade levels below the norm of the state. The causes of the academic problems of these students can stem from problems in the home to mild medical conditions. The RSP student will usually attend one or two regular classes along with several specially designed classes are part of the Special Ed program to give them extra help. This student, for all purposes is normal functioning, and sometimes is embarrassed or shocked that he or she has been placed in a RSP class. (It is normally a good idea to keep the doors closed during these classes as these students prefer anonymity whenever possible.) This is termed mild Special Ed.

## The SDC Class

The second category of Special Ed is the SDC or Special Day Class. This category of Special Ed class is where the students have fallen to 3 or 4 grade levels below the states norm. The level of emotional func-

*"Whate'er we leave to God, God does and blesses us."–*
*Henry David Thoreau*

149

tioning and learning ability is even more problematic at this stage. The SDC student is given even more help than the RSP student, and as with all Special Ed classes, the class size is small and usually limited to about 10 students. This class is often called moderate Special Ed.

In all Special Ed classes a potpourri of subjects are taught within the hour that the students are there: math, history, reading, writing and spelling. These courses are designed with a remedial perspective to help the student, if possible, catch up to the norm for his or her grade level and age group.

## The MT Special Ed Class

Of all the Special Ed categories, the one that requires the most patience, skill, compassion and professionalism is the MT (mentally retarded) Special Ed class which is classified as severe. In this class, you will find students with genetic defects, severe learning disabilities, autism and emotional disorders where students must be monitored by psychiatrists who prescribe them appropriate medications to function in normal classroom situations. These classes are always taught under the Special Education department of the school.

## The IEP

The IEP (Individualized Education Program) is a long and detailed write up sometimes comprising of more than 25 pages, depending on the severity of the case, which details the problem and developmental history for each student participating in the Special Ed program. The IEP is written and filed away by the regular Special Ed teacher. If it were really necessary, you would have access to these files to learn about any student that you would have under your temporary substitute teaching care.

Were you to need to look up an IEP on any particular student, you would go and read the most current summary which could be found in Section E entitled "Present Level of Performance". Generally speaking, the IEP is done to state the goals for achievement that are set for each student and to have a record which is done periodically to restate if the set goals are being met and what remedial measures would be necessary to implement.

## Your TA is Your Best Friend

With all of that said about the degree of specialty of the Special Ed class, IEP's and all of the possible behavior problems of the Special Ed student, I have very good news for you. You will never have to teach a Special Ed class without help, and the classes are generally very small in size, usually less than ten students. Your absolute greatest resource to a successful day substituting in a Special Ed class is your TA (teacher's

*"Do what you can, with what you have, where you are."—Theodore Roosevelt*

assistant). She (or he, though usually it's a she) after almost the first five minutes, begins to take on the appearance of a superhero. Your TA knows intimately the behavior of each student. She can tell you where the IEP's are and the particulars of any student there. The TA usually has earned the respect of the students to such a degree that his or her control on their bad behavior is remarkable. TA's tend to be very proactive and take-charge type of professionals. They know who the students are, what the procedures are, what the lesson plan is and are willing to do whatever is necessary to make your job much easier. Lean on their knowledge and skills as much as you can. That is why they are there, and this is what they love to do. With a good TA at your side, your day can be made much easier and more gratifying.

*"If you don't stand for something, you'll fall for anything."–Michael Evans*

*"Shoot for the moon, even if you miss, you will land among the stars."* —Les Brown

# How to Teach Gifted Students

With all the talk of discipline problems and difficult students, there is a pleasant delight of a class that you will sooner or later teach as a substitute teacher, and that is the gifted or high achievers class. Because of very high scores on certain entrance and placement exams, all of these students are placed in a special class called gifted. They are very proud of their elite status, and they abhor the idea of being compared or associated with the "oridinary/misbehaving" students.

As a group, they are very smart and well-behaved. I don't know, it appears like refinement and good manners are concomitant and go hand in hand with educated minds. Once they know what their assignment is, they then go pretty much on automatic pilot. They are usually independent workers and proactive, once they know what the lesson plan is. You know, come to think of it, I don't think I've ever raised my voice while teaching in a gifted class. Now this doesn't mean that you will never have a discipline problem. They are only mild in comparison to the regular classes and are few and far in between.

## You Still Have to Be Firm

High IQ kids sometimes can be moody or temperamental. If you have a problem with any kid, it will probably be with one who is a master at sarcasm or verbal repartee.

"Is that the answer, Joseph?"

"Well, it all depends on what <u>is</u>, <i>is?</i>"

"Look, if you don't finish the problem, I will tell your teacher..."

"Okay, I'm sorry, Mr. Prosper. I'll finish it right away."

That's all you need in a gifted class, and they get right back on track. So, be firm in spite of their high IQ's. Remember, that it is in these classes where you will find all the brilliant future doctors, politicians and crooked lawyers.

Once you give them their assignment and they know what to do, you can relax, maybe even read a book as you casually and intermittently look up and walk around to see that they are on task.

Once you find a teacher who has one of these type of classes, of gifted, refined, hard-working and high achieving students, you want to do whatever it takes for this teacher to call you in next time and every time. Give them a thank you note–with a $40 fine-restaurant gift card.

*"Strength is a matter of the made-up mind."–John Beecher*

*"Shoot for the moon, even if you miss, you will land among the stars."*–Les Brown

# Pros and Cons of Long Term Subbing

When you talk to someone who is considering becoming a day-by-day substitute teacher, one of the first things that comes up is the question of security. How secure is a substitute teaching position. Well, my response to that is always that it is as secure as you make it by design, that is, it is as secure as you diligently and conscientiously promote yourself in two or three schools that you have selected as prime. Nevertheless, you will come across the opportunity to take on and sub on a long-term assignment. Essentially, a long term assignment is when you are offered the chance to teach in the same classroom, in the same school and with the same kids for usually 30 consecutive days. As with any choice, there are advantages and disadvantages. Before you take on any long term sub assignment, consider these pros and cons first, and you will thus make a much better decision.

*"One arrow does not bring down two birds."—Turkish proverb*

### The 4 Advantages of Long Term Subbing:
- Guaranteed Work Days
- Guaranteed Daily Pay
- Pay at a Higher Rate
- Discover What It's Like to Be a Full-Time Teacher

### The 6 Disadvantages of Long Term Subbing:
- May Get <u>Stuck</u> with a <u>Horrible</u> Class for 4 Weeks
- Must Do Lesson Plans
- Must Create Tests
- Must Do Grading
- Must Go to Administrative Meetings
- Out of the Promotional Loop for 4 Weeks

We've all heard the saying, "One man's meat is another man's poison." Well, that is sort of going to be the case as to how an advantage or disadvantage might be taken. If you are a dedicated sub with his or her eye set on the goal of becoming a full time teacher, then most of the disadvantages will, for you, be advantages. Conversely, if you are a lifelong dedicated full-time professional substitute teacher with other interests and activities outside of substitute teaching that you enjoy doing equally as well, then the extra time that you must spend to do a long term position, for you, would then make it a disadvantage. I am assuming that most of you who are reading this book is because you like the idea primarily of subbing versus a full-time permanent position, and based on this premise will we call advantages and disadvantages as such. First let us look at the 4 advantages:

### Advantage #1 - Guaranteed Work Days

The tenuous position of day-to-day subbing is not always knowing where your work is going to come from in the next several weeks. Not so with a long term position. You know for sure that you are going to be working, everyday, for the next 4 weeks, and there is no guessing as to where your assignments will come from.

### Advantage #2 - Guaranteed Pay

If you work everyday, then the concomitant advantage is that your earnings are guaranteed everyday for the next 30 days. At least for a month, you can boast of guaranteed job security.

### Advantage #3 - Pay at a Higher Rate

In most school districts, you are paid at a higher daily rate for working 30 consecutive days in a row on a long term position, or you are given an extra check as a bonus. In some parts of the country, the bonus could be from an extra $500 to $1000 for working 30 days in a row on a long term substitute teacher.

### Advantage #4 - Discover What It's Like to Be Full-Time

I'm really not sure if this is an advantage or a disadvantage. It all depends on what your goals are. If you definitely are considering to be a full-time permanent teacher in the future, then this is definitely your opportunity to preview and experience what it would to be like. If you really don't want to ever become a permanent full-time teacher, then this "advantage" will be rather moot.

Alright, let's take a look at the disadvantages:

### Disadvantage #1 - May Get Stuck with a Nightmare Class

When it comes to taking long term positions, I am very cautious about it. I know for a fact that many long term positions open up because of a "burn out" factor. What I mean is that some classes are so bad that the regular teacher just decides to take a hiatus and call it quits for a month. These are usually special ed classes, mild to moderate, with emotional disturbed students with lots of self-control issues. If possible try to meet the teacher, and check out the class at least once before you accept it. You don't need a long term nightmare.

*"Nothing is really work unless you'd rather be doing something else."—Anonymous*

### Disadvantage #2 - Must Do Lesson Plans

Assuming that you don't want to be a full-time permanent teacher and assuming that you have other things that you enjoy doing when you get off of work from a day of teaching, doing lesson plans will definitely bite into you evening free time. Not much. Maybe an hour or less, but it is still time you would have had to spend doing something that will take away from your other occupations.

### Disadvantage #3 - Must Create Tests

Creating tests again involves time out of your evenings, and this is something that you must create because students should be tested on their progress at least twice a week.

### Disadvantage #4 - Must Do Grading

Now grading *is* time-consuming. Let us say that you have six periods with 35 students in each class. That's a total of 210 students and a total of 420 quizzes or tests that you must correct each week and then *enter* the grades into the teacher's grade book. If it takes you, for example, 2 minutes to correct each student's quiz or test and then enter the grade into the teacher's grade book, then you would have to spend 840 minutes per week or *14 additional hours per week!* You are, of course, being paid extra for this, but some people value their free time even more than money. You must decide.

*"When love and skill work together, expect a masterpiece."*–John Ruskin

### Disadvantage #5 - Must Go to Administrative Meetings

If you ever want to hear a grown man or woman moan and cry, just tell a teacher that they have to go to a series of administrative departmental meetings. Depending on who's giving them, these meetings are extremely useful and beneficial, or, they are extremely boring and a waste of time. Many suicides have occurred during departmental administrative meetings.

### Disadvantage #6 - Out of the Promotional Loop for Weeks

As a substitute teacher, you must never forget that you are a free agent and that you are in business for yourself, the business and service of being a substitute teacher for as many teachers and schools as possible. Your schools and your teachers who call on you on a regular basis are your customers. Once you take on a long term position, you severe your connections with your regular customers for a month. When they call on you, you are not available, and like any client, if they can't get services from you, they will go somewhere else. You are getting them use to calling on other subs during this time. The front office girls that are used to calling on you, will discover that you are unavailable for a month. You can reestablish yourself again, but you may lose a few clients.

*"Shoot for the moon, even if you miss, you will land among the stars."*—Les Brown

# Subbing State by State

In chapter 3, I spent a lot of time talking about how to qualify to work in California by taking the CBEST test. When there are any other similar type tests that must be taken in other states, the study technique for taking the CBEST test could be easily applied to any other type state qualifying test. However, I am well aware that California is not the center of the world, nor does every future sub reside there. Recognizing this, I have listed for you the contact information for the departments of education, state by state, in order to for you to be able to call them directly on becoming a substitute teacher in your area.

I have taken a sample city and a sample school district, and have listed the salary for that particular district, but keep in mine that within any state, there are seemingly countless school districts, and to cover what the pay scale is for each and every school district is way beyond the scope of this work. I was able to obtain more complete information from some states more than others. (My next book will cover an exhaustive list of every school district's pay scale of every state.) Also keep in mind that requirements and pay scale change from time to time. The tendency is always for salaries to increase; this is why I have listed the state departments' contact information and web site for you to get the latest pay and educational requirements for your state and the district you are interested in working in.

Most schools have subs work 6 hours, 6.6 hours or 7 hours per work day. (Becoming a full-time credentialed teacher is a whole different ball of wax with a completely different set of educational requirements.) Please keep in mind that here in this chapter we talking about the minimum requirements, state by state, for a *substitute teaching certificate*. This information is to be a ***substitute teacher only***!

## Links to State Education Agencies

In doing this research on the departments of education for each state of the United States, I came across a fabulous web site which with one click, links you to every state department of education in the country.

`http://www.nasbe.org/SEA_Links/SEA_Links.html`

Now, let's see where it is that you need to contact to find about subbing in whatever state you happen to reside:

*"God's ear lies close to the believer's lip."–Anonymous*

159

**Alabama** Dept. of Education
50 North Ripley Street
P.O. Box 302101
Montgomery, AL 36104
Phone: (334) 242-9700
http://www.alsde.edu/

Minimum Education Requirement:
B.A.:  no (only two years college)
Specialized Test:  no
Sample Salary:
Birmingham, AL
$60.00 per day
$8.00 per hour  (7.5-hour workday)
$125.00 day after 20 long term days

**Alaska** Dept. of Education
801 West 10th Street
Suite 200
Juneau, AK 99801-1878
Telephone: (907) 465-2800
Fax: (907) 465-4156
http://www.eed.state.ak.us/

Minimum Education Requirement:
B.A.:  yes
Specialized Test:  no (Only attend a 1
week training.)
Sample Salary:
Fairbanks, AK
$90.00 per day (starting salary)
$12.85 per hour  (7-hour workday)
After 140 hours experience = $16.43
per hour or $115.00 per day

*"To play it safe is not to
play."–Robert Altman*

**Arizona** Dept. of Education
1535 West Jefferson Street
Phoenix, AZ 85007
Phone: (602) 542-5393
1(800) 352-4558 (Arizona)
http://www.ade.az.gov/

Minimum Education Requirement:
B.A.:  yes
Specialized Test:  no
Sample Salary:
Phoenix, AZ
$70.00 per day (One 5-hour shift)
$14.00 per hour  (5-hour workday
with the possibility of working two 5-
hour shifts thus doubling daily salary. )

**Arkansas** Dept. of Education
#4 Capital Mall
Little Rock, AR 72201
Phone: (501) 682-4475
http://arkedu.state.ar.us/

**California** Dept. of Education
1430 N Street
Sacramento, CA 95814
916-319-0800
http://www.cde.ca.gov/

Minimum Education Requirement:
B.A.:  yes
Specialized Test:  yes,  CBEST test
Sample Salary:
Los Angeles  $172.00 per day
$26.00 per hour  (6.6-hour workday)
$1,105.00 after 20 long term days

**Colorado** Dept. of Education
State Office Building
201 East Colfax Avenue
Denver, CO 80203-1799
Phone: (303) 866-6600
Fax: (303) 830-0793
http://www.cde.state.co.us/

Minimum Education Requirement:
B.A.: yes     (3 yr. sub authorization)
Specialized Test:  no
Sample Salary:
Denver, CO
$81.20 per day
$10.15 per hour  (8-hour workday)
$153.21 day after 17 long term days

**Connecticut** Dept. of Education
Office of Communications
165 Capitol Avenue
Hartford CT 06145
Phone: (860) 713-6969
http://www.state.ct.us/sde/

*"As soon as you trust your-self, you will know how to live."–Johann von Goethe*

**Delaware** Dept. of Education
Townsend Building
401 Federal St., Suite 2
Dover, DE 19901
Phone: (302) 739-4601
Fax: (302) 739-4654
http://www.doe.state.de.us/

**Florida** Dept. of Education
Turlington Building
325 West Gaines Street
Suite 1514
Tallahassee, FL 32399
Phone: (850) 245-0505
Fax: (850) 245-9667
http://www.fldoe.org/

Minimum Education Requirement:
B.A.:  yes  (with 2.5 GPA)
Specialized Test:  no
Sample Salary:
Miami, FL
$87.00 per day

**Georgia** Dept. of Education
2054 Twin Towers East
Atlanta, Georgia 30334
Phone:  (404) 656-2800
1(800) 311-3627 (GA)
Fax: (404) 651-6867
http://www.doe.k12.ga.us/

**Guam** Dept. of Education
Attn: Personnel Services Division
P.O. Box DE
Hagåtña, Guam  96932
Phone: (671) 475-0495
Fax: (671) 477-0698
http://www.cde.state.co.us/

**Hawaii** Dept. of Education
P.O. Box 2360
Honolulu, HI 96804
Phone: (808) 586-3349
Fax: (808) 586-3433
http://doe.k12.hi.us/

Minimum Education Requirement:
B.A.:   yes
Specialized Test:  no (30-hr. training)
Sample Salary:
Honolulu, HI
$112.53 per day
$16.07 per hour  (7-hour workday)

**Idaho** Dept. of Education
650 West State Street
PO Box 83720
Boise, ID  83720-0027
Phone: (208) 332-6800
http://www.sde.state.id.us/Dept/

*"Trust in God and do something."–Mary Lyon*

**Illinois** Dept. of Education
100 N. 1st Street
Springfield, IL  62777
Phone: (866) 262-6663
http://www.isbe.state.il.us/

**Indiana** Dept. of Education
Room 229, State House
Indianapolis, IN 46204-2798
Phone: (317) 232-6610
Fax: (317) 232-8004
http://doe.state.in.us/

**Iowa** Dept. of Education
Grimes State Office Building
400 East 14th Street
Des Moines, IA 50319-0146
Phone: (515) 281-5294
Fax: (515) 242-5988
http://www.cde.state.co.us/

**Kansas** Dept. of Education
120 SE 10th Avenue
Topeka KS 66612-1182
Phone: (785) 296-3201
Fax: (785) 296-7933
http://www.ksbe.state.ks.us/

*"My belief is God unto my-
self."–Charles Prosper*

**Kentucky** Dept. of Education
500 Mero Street, 19th Floor
Frankfort, KY  40601
Phone: (502) 564-3421
Fax: (502) 564-6470
http://www.cde.state.co.us/

**Louisiana** Dept. of Education
P.O. Box 94064
Baton Rouge, LA  70804-9064
Phone: (225) 342-3490
Fax: (303) 830-0793
http://www.doe.state.la.us/

Minimum Education Requirement:
B.A.:   no (only high school diploma)
Specialized Test:  no
Sample Salary:
New Orleans, LA
$49.98 per day
$8.33 per hour  (6-hour workday)

**Maine** Dept. of Education
23 State House Station
 Augusta, ME  80203-1799
Phone: (207) 624-6600
Fax: (207) 624-6800
http://www.state.me.us/educa-
tion/

**Maryland** Dept. of Education
200 W. Baltimore Street
Baltimore, MD  21201
Phone: (410) 767-0019
http://www.marylandpublic-schools.org/msde

Minimum Education Requirement:
B.A.:  yes
Specialized Test:  no
Sample Salary:
Westminster, MD
$90.00 per day

**Massachusetts** Dept. of Education
350 Main Street
Malden, MA 02148-5023
(781)338-3000
http://www.doe.mass.edu/

*"Luck is believing you're lucky."*–Tennessee Williams

**Michigan** Dept. of Education
608 W. Allegan Street
P.O. Box 30008
Lansing, MI  48909
Phone: (517) 373-3324
http://www.michigan.gov/mde

**Minnesota** Dept. of Education
1500 Highway 36 West
Roseville, MN 55113-4266
Phone: (651) 582-8200
http://education.state.mn.us/html/mde_home.htm

**Mississippi** Dept. of Education
Central High School
P.O. Box 771
359 North West Street
Jackson, MS 39205
Phone: (601) 359-3513
http://www.mde.k12.ms.us/

**Missouri** Dept. of Education
PO Box 480
Jefferson City, MO 65102
Phone: (573) 751-4212
Fax: (573) 751-8613
http://www.dese.state.mo.us/

**Montana** Dept. of Education
P.O. Box 202501
Helena, MT 59620-2501
Phone:  (406) 444-3095
http://www.opi.state.mt.us/

*"Self-trust is the first secret of success."–Ralph Waldo Emerson*

**Nebraska** Dept. of Education
301 Centennial Mall South
P.O. Box 94987
Lincoln, NE  68509
Phone: (402) 471-2295
http://www.nde.state.ne.us/

Minimum Education Requirement:
B.A.:   no (only 60 semester hours)
Specialized Test:  no
Sample Salary:
Omaha, NE
$140.00 per day

**Nevada** Dept. of Education
Carson City Main Location
700 E. Fifth Street
Carson City, NV 89701
Phone: (775) 687-9200
Fax: (775) 687-9101
http://www.doe.nv.gov/

**New Hamphire** Dept. of Education
101 Pleasant Street
201 East Colfax Avenue
Concord, NH 03301-3860
Phone: (603) 271-3494
Fax: (603) 271-1953
http://www.ed.state.nh.us/education/

New Jersey Dept. of Education
P.O. Box 500
Trenton, NJ 08625
Phone: (609) 292-4469
http://www.state.nj.us/education/

New Mexico Dept. of Education
300 Don Gaspar
Santa Fe, NM  87501-2786
Phone: (505) 827-5800
http://sde.state.nm.us/

*"Never stop.  One always stops as soon as something is about to happen."–Peter Brook*

New York Dept. of Education
89 Washington Avenue
Albany, New York 12234
Phone: (518) 474-3901
http://www.nysed.gov/

Minimum Education Requirement:
B.A.:   yes
Specialized Test:  yes   NYSTCE
Sample Salary:
New York, New York
$129.00 per day
$19.37 per hour  (6.6-hour workday)

North Carolina Dept. of Education
6302 Mail Service Center
201 East Colfax Avenue
Raleigh, NC 27699-6302
Phone: (919) 807-3304
Fax: (919) 807-3198
http://www.dpi.state.nc.us/

North Dakota Dept. of Education
600 E. Boulevard Ave.
Dept. 201  Floors 9, 10 and 11
Bismarck, ND  58505-0440
Phone: (701) 328-2260
Fax: (701) 328-2461
http://www.dpi.state.nd.us/

**Ohio** Dept. of Education
25 South Front Street
Columbus, OH 43215-4183
Phone: (877) 644-6338
http://www.ode.state.oh.us/

**Oklahoma** Dept. of Education
2500 North Lincoln Boulevard
Oklahoma City, OK 73105-
4599
Phone: (405) 521-3301
Fax: (405) 521-6205
http://www.sde.state.ok.us/

*"Many of life's failures are men who did not realize how close they were to success when they gave up."*–*Thomas Alva Edison*

**Oregon** Dept. of Education
255 Capitol Street NE
Salem, OR 97310-0203
Phone: (503) 378-3569
Fax: (503) 378-5156
http://www.ode.state.or.us/

**Pennysylania** Dept. of Education
333 Market Street
Harrisburg, PA  17126
Phone: (717) 783-6788
http://www.pde.state.pa.us/

**Rhode Island** Dept. of Education
255 Westminster Street
Providence, RI 02903
Phone: (401) 222-4600
http://www.ridoe.net/

**South Carolina** Dept. of Education
1429 Senate Street
Columbia, SC 29201
Phone: (803) 734-8500
Fax: (803) 734-3389
http://www.myscschools.com/

**South Dakota** Dept. of Education
700 Governors Drive
Pierre, SD 57501-2291
Phone: (605) 773-3553
Fax: (605) 773-6139
http://www.state.sd.us/deca/

*"Fear knocked at the door. Faith answered. And lo, no one was there."–Anonymous*

**Tennessee** Dept. of Education
Andrew Johnson Tower
9th Floor
710 James Robertson Parkway
Nashville, TN 37243-1050
Phone: (615) 741-2966
Fax: (615) 741-0371
http://www.state.tn.us/education/

**Texas** Dept. of Education
1701 North Congress Avenue
Austin, Texas, 78701
Phone: (512) 463-9734
http://www.tea.state.tx.us/

**Utah** Dept. of Education
250 East 500 South
P. O. Box 144200
Salt Lake City, UT 84114
Phone: (801) 538-7500
http://www.usoe.k12.ut.us/

**Vermont** Dept. of Education
120 State Street
Montpelier, VT 05620-2501
Phone: (802) 828-2445
http://www.state.vt.us/educ/

**Virginia** Dept. of Education
James Monroe Building
101 N. 14th Street
Richmond, VA 23219
Phone: 1 (800) 292-3820
http://www.pen.k12.va.us/

*"A strong passion for any object will guarantee success, for the desire of the end will point to the means."–William Hazlitt*

**Washingtom D.C.** Dept. of Education
825 North Capitol Street, NE
7th Floor
Washington, D.C., 20002
Phone: (202) 724-4222
http://www.k12.dc.us/dcps/
home.html

**Washington** Dept. of Education
Old Capitol Building
P. O. Box 47200
Olympia, WA 98504-7200
Phone: (360) 725-6000
http://www.k12.wa.us/

**West Virginia** Dept. of Education
1900 Kanawha Boulevard East
Building 6, Room 252
Charleston, WV 25305
Phone: (304) 558-7842
Fax: (304) 558-7843
http://wvde.state.wv.us/

**Wisconsin** Dept. of Education
125 S. Webster St.
PO Box 7841
Madison, WI 53707-7841
Phone: 1 (800) 441-4563
http://www.dpi.state.wi.us/

**Wyoming** Dept. of Education
2300 Capitol Avenue
Hathaway Building, 2nd Floor
Cheyenne, WY 82002-0050
Phone: (307) 777-7675
http://www.k12.wy.us/

*"Obstacles are those frightful things you see when you take your eyes off the goal."–Hannah More*

## Working As A Sub in Your State

In the handful of examples of the salaries and minimum educational requirements that I have listed, you will notice that there is a great disparity from one state to another. Salaries and educational requirements change from year to year and from district to district within each state. The first thing that I would suggest for you is to go to your particular state department of education's web site, and read everything that they have already listed concerning the state and the district where you want to work as a sub.

The next thing that you will have to do is to get on the phone and talk to a real live person, in the department of certification for substitute teachers. You must ask specifically what is the current minimum education requirements to be a *sub*. Don't be surprised if they go off on a tangent and start talking to you about the requirements for a permanent teacher's credential. If you are not interested in working as a permanent full-time teacher, you must make it clear to them that you what information to work as a substitute teacher only. Ask them specifically what is the salary per hour in their district and how many hours constitute a teacher's work day. You must also ask if they pay more for a long term assignment which usually is an assignment where you teach in the same school and the same class for 20 consecutive work days. Ask if they pay health and insurance benefits for you and your family; so school districts pay benefits, some don't. You have to ask.

Most importantly, I would suggest that you go around to 3 or 4 schools in the area where you want to work and go in to the main offices and introduce yourself and ask if they have a sub list where they call regular subs. Your purpose of going in to the main offices is to also ask for the names of phone number of a couple of their top subs at their school because you would like to speak to them to get their advice on how to be a good sub. You also want to know a little bit about the student body, the area and the school politics. Keep in mind that whatever the regular subs tell you, you must take it with a grain of salt. Some subs are just whiners and complainers, while others, the super subs will give you a more positive perspective of the school. If the salary and pay scale is not what you want in a particular school district, don't let that stop you, investigate the adjacent and adjoining school districts of your area to see if there is any difference. The key thing to keep in mind is to know what you want, stay positive and keep looking until you find what you want.

*"We are Divine Personalities as part of God's divine dream of Himself."–Charles Prosper*

*"Shoot for the moon, even if you miss, you will land among the stars."*—Les Brown

# The Future of Substitute Teaching

It is up to the collective consciousness and performance of all substitute teachers around the country to raise the perception and the importance of what we do as substitute teachers. We are _teachers_–not just "subs". We perform and indispensable service in the absence of the regular full-time teachers.

### (NASST) National Association of Super Substitute Teachers

As you read these words, there is a growing body of a new breed of substitute teachers as part of a new organization which I have spearheaded, the National Association of Super Substitute Teachers (NASST) whose aim is to better the working conditions, the salaries and the benefits of all substitute teachers around the country. We are a network of substitute teachers, labor organizers, lawyers and influential politicians who together can help us achieve higher and higher goals in the _profession_ of substitute teaching. If you would like to become a member and/or contribute your special skills and influence, please contact:

> Charles Prosper _(President)_
> NASST _(National Association of Super Substitute Teachers)_
> P.O. Box 29699
> Los Angeles, CA 90029-0699
> (323) 662-7841 _phone_
> (323) 644-8221 _fax_
> _cprosper@supersubstitute.com_

On behalf of the entire teaching profession and all of the parents who want the best for their kids in the public schools, we thank you for your contribution. Enjoy your kids. Enjoy your life.

_"Be like a postage stamp–stick to one thing until you get there."–Josh Billings_

CHAPTER
14

**CHARLES PROSPER, B.A.,** is an author of 5 books, lecturer and researcher who has had more than seven years of full-time real life substitute teaching in the most challenging of middle and high schools in the Los Angeles Unified School District. He is the one who first became to be known an SuperSub. His subject specialty is Spanish, computer graphics, English and science. He is one of the most requested substitute teachers in Los Angeles County, so much that he is usually booked to work in one or two choice schools for a much as two months solid in advance.

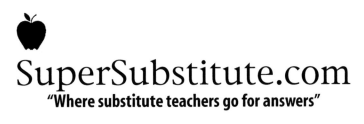

SuperSubstitute.com
"Where substitute teachers go for answers"

# 🍎 Quick & Easy Order Form

**Yes, please rush me the following items:**

❑ The Super Sub Solution (Book)..............................................................................$35.00

❑ The Super Sub Solution (2 Instructional Audio CD's)........................................$27.00

❑ The Super Sub Solution (DVD program 30 min.)..............................................$35.00

**Shipping by Air U.S.:** $4.00 for first book or disk and $2.00 for each additional product. _____

**Sales Tax:** Please add 8.25% for products shipped to California addresses. _____

**TOTAL OF ORDER** _____

**Please send more FREE information on:**

❑ Other Books  ❑ Other Audios  ❑ Other DVD's  ❑ Seminars  ❑ Newsletters  ❑ Reports

❑ Please charge my credit card: ❑ Mastercard  ❑ Visa  ❑ Amex  ❑ Discover  ❑ Diners Club

_____            _____

Credit Card #                                                          Exp. Date

_____            _____

Name as it appears on card                                        Signature

_____

The last three security digits on back of credit card       ❑ Check            ❑ Money Order

Name _____

Address _____

City _____ State _____ Zip _____

Daytime Phone # _____

*(in case we have a question on your order)*

Email _____

Email, call, mail or fax to:        Charles Prosper
Global Publishing Company
P.O. Box 29699
Los Angeles, CA 90029-0699
cprosper@supersubstitute.com
(323) 662-7841 *phone*
(323) 644-8221 *fax*
**www.supersubstitute.com**

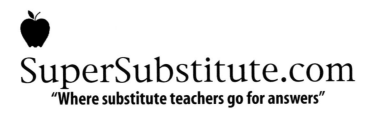

SuperSubstitute.com
"Where substitute teachers go for answers"

# 🍎 Quick & Easy Order Form

**Yes, please rush me the following items:**

❑ The Super Sub Solution (Book)...........................................................................$35.00

❑ The Super Sub Solution (2 Instructional Audio CD's).......................................$27.00

❑ The Super Sub Solution (DVD program 30 min.)..............................................$35.00

**Shipping by Air U.S.:** $4.00 for first book or disk and $2.00 for each additional product. _____

**Sales Tax:** Please add 8.25% for products shipped to California addresses. _____

**TOTAL OF ORDER** _____

**Please send more FREE information on:**

❑ Other Books   ❑ Other Audios   ❑ Other DVD's   ❑ Seminars   ❑ Newsletters   ❑ Reports

❑ Please charge my credit card: ❑Mastercard   ❑Visa   ❑Amex   ❑Discover   ❑Diners Club

_____          _____
Credit Card #                                                              Exp. Date

_____          _____
Name as it appears on card                                       Signature

_____
The last three security digits on back of credit card        ❑ Check        ❑ Money Order

Name _____

Address _____

City _____ State _____ Zip _____

Daytime Phone # _____
*(in case we have a question on your order)*

Email _____

Email, call, mail or fax to:      Charles Prosper
Global Publishing Company
P.O. Box 29699
Los Angeles, CA 90029-0699
cprosper@supersubstitute.com
(323) 662-7841 *phone*
(323) 644-8221 *fax*
**www.supersubstitute.com**

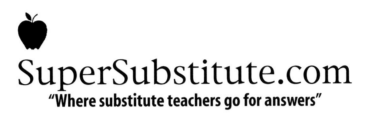

SuperSubstitute.com
"Where substitute teachers go for answers"

# 🍎 Quick & Easy Order Form

**Yes, please rush me the following items:**

❑ The Super Sub Solution (Book).................................................................$35.00

❑ The Super Sub Solution (2 Instructional Audio CD's).........................$27.00

❑ The Super Sub Solution (DVD program 30 min.).................................$35.00

**Shipping by Air U.S.:** $4.00 for first book or disk and $2.00 for each additional product. _____

**Sales Tax:** Please add 8.25% for products shipped to California addresses. _____

**TOTAL OF ORDER** _____

**Please send more FREE information on:**

❑ Other Books   ❑ Other Audios   ❑ Other DVD's   ❑ Seminars   ❑ Newsletters   ❑ Reports

❑ Please charge my credit card: ❑Mastercard   ❑Visa   ❑Amex   ❑Discover   ❑Diners Club

_____            _____

Credit Card #                                                                          Exp. Date

_____            _____

Name as it appears on card                                                      Signature

_____

The last three security digits on back of credit card            ❑ Check            ❑ Money Order

Name _____

Address _____

City _____ State _____ Zip _____

Daytime Phone # _____
*(in case we have a question on your order)*

Email _____

Email, call, mail or fax to:   Charles Prosper
Global Publishing Company
P.O. Box 29699
Los Angeles, CA 90029-0699
cprosper@supersubstitute.com
(323) 662-7841 *phone*
(323) 644-8221 *fax*
**www.supersubstitute.com**